BLESS YOUR HEART

V.W. Thomack

ARCHWAY
PUBLISHING

Archway Publishing books may be ordered through booksellers or by contacting:

Archway Publishing
1663 Liberty Drive
Bloomington, IN 47403
www.archwaypublishing.com
844-669-3957

Because of the dynamic nature of the Internet, any web addresses or
links contained in this book may have changed since publication and
may no longer be valid. The views expressed in this work are solely those
of the author and do not necessarily reflect the views of the publisher,
and the publisher hereby disclaims any responsibility for them.

Any people depicted in stock imagery provided by Getty Images are
models, and such images are being used for illustrative purposes only.
Certain stock imagery © Getty Images.

ISBN: 978-1-6657-2014-4 (sc)
ISBN: 978-1-6657-2012-0 (hc)
ISBN: 978-1-6657-2013-7 (e)

Library of Congress Control Number: 2022904469

Print information available on the last page.

Archway Publishing rev. date: 03/25/2022

PREFACE

When I first thought of writing a book, I had no intention of writing about myself, but rather about certain characters who were part of my life in one way or another. However, there's no way to do that without involving myself. I think that's good, because it allows me to express regrets regarding several issues that I should have reacted to but didn't. I regard these as failures and have carried them in my heart and on my mind for years.

More than likely, a number of changes that impacted people negatively would not have occurred had I done my duty, and I apologize for that. Of course, one can't change the past, but if I were able to, I'd try to be a better husband, father, and person.

I'm not an author or a novelist, so don't get your expectations too high. I will follow a chronological path for the most part. However, because of the nature of an issue, I may jump ahead at times to complete a story. Also, I will stay with given names only for the most part. Some names are actual, while others are fictitious. All events are true according to my recollection.

Warning: I'll be interjecting some jokes here and there. Some might be considered off-color, but please take these for what they are—just jokes for a change of pace and, hopefully, a few good laughs.

CHAPTER 1

27

Helen and her very good friend, Donna, were having a heavenly lunch when they were abruptly interrupted by Sheila, an old class-mate of Helen's she hadn't seen in years. Sheila gushed, "Oh, darling, did you know I married Adrian Atherton, the real estate mogul?"

Helen replied, "Well, bless your heart."

Sheila went on, "He's so wonderful to me. He gave me a five-carat emerald-cut diamond for our first anniversary."

Again, Helen replied, "Well, bless your heart."

Sheila continued to ignore Donna and said, "Adrian gave me a new Mercedes-Benz for my birthday this year."

Helen cheerfully reacted with, "Well, bless your heart."

> Sheila glanced at her watch and declared, "Oh dear, I'm going to be late for our meeting to plan a cruise around the world."
>
> Helen blessed Sheila again as she flounced away.
>
> Donna watched her leave and asked Helen, "How could you be so sweet to that woman?"
>
> Helen smiled and said, "Oh, I really wasn't. You see, my husband sent me to charm school shortly after were married, and 'Bless your heart' is charm-school language for 'Who gives a shit.'"

My mother, Anna Ida, was born on October 27, and she delivered me at 8:08 a.m. on March 27. My dad always recalled they'd had the worst blizzard that day, and back then, blizzards were more common. I've seen pictures of snow banks as high as the telephone wires on some country roads.

Nothing of note happened on a 27th until I got married on November 27, 1954, the Saturday after Thanksgiving. I didn't select the date. Note that *54* is two times *27*. It would be some time before another 27th event happened, and they'd come relatively rapidly thereafter.

My wife and I were returning home from visiting a neighbor, Mary Richardson, two doors away. We were there to express our condolences for the tragic death of her husband, Jesse, who was a major in the army and, I believe, an ROTC instructor at the University of Kentucky. He was driving home late one evening when he apparently fell asleep at the wheel. He hit a guardrail, which punched through the grill and dashboard of his vehicle, impaling him.

My wife and I had three children: Julie, Scott, and Stephanie. It was as we were returning home from the Richardsons' house that I told my wife I wanted another son. We were blessed with John on the following August 27. This had nothing to do with our visit to Mrs. Richardson. It's just that it marked the time I aired the desire to hopefully have another son.

In time, John got married, and his first child, Lindsay, was born on February 27, followed by Cassie Mae on May 27 of the following year. Somehow, Emily Jo arrived on a different date, as did the fourth daughter, Molly, whom he had with his second wife. I thought something was amiss and added the last two birthdays together, thinking the total would be another 27.

When John and his first wife divorced, they agreed to stay on friendly terms for the sake of the children, but that friendship was often strained by her constant visits to her attorney to seek more money for alimony and child support. John determined that he would never marry again, even after he met a wonderful woman, Patti, on a blind date. But that all changed when they were flying to New York and the pilot announced they would be cruising at 27,000 feet. That magic number compelled John to drop to his knee and propose marriage right then and there. They married on December 27. John has adopted 27 and has it tattooed on his arm. His auto vanity plate is TWNTSVN.

My granddaughter, Lindsay, has my wedding date, 11/27/54, tattooed on her ankle. This past September, there was a big wedding reception for her in her parents' spacious backyard. I thought it strange that no seating was set up in the tent. About the time the ceremony was expected to start, John called for everyone's attention and announced there wouldn't be one. He'd become an ordained minister via the internet and had performed the ceremony earlier in the year on March 27, which was unknown even to me at the time. The reception had been delayed because of COVID-19.

My granddaughter Cassie Mae had been married two years earlier on June 27, and I was asked to do the prayer part. I preceded that with a recount of the 27 happenings, lastly noting that my only brother had died two years before on this very date. I was going to tell a joke about having children, but I skipped it, as I had already been onstage too long.

My granddaughter Anna had been married three or four years earlier. She was in the navy, where she'd met Brian, an avid Ohio State Buckeyes die-hard. I am the same for the Wisconsin Badgers. It must have irked Brian mightily when Bucky Badger appeared at the wedding reception and I did a jig with him. Well, Brian got his oar in the water first, as Buckeyes had been served at the rehearsal dinner. I was asked to do the prayer for the wedding dinner and surprised everyone by singing "Go My Children with My Blessing." I couldn't believe the cheering and clapping by the guests as they rose to their feet.

Go my children with my blessing … you are never alone
Waking, sleeping I am with you … you are my own.
In my love's baptismal river I have made you mine forever
Go my children, with my blessing, you are my own.
In this union I have joined you, husband and wife.
Now my children, live together as heirs of life.
Each the other's gladness sharing, each the other's burdens bearing.
Now my children, live together as heirs of life.
I the Lord will bless and keep you and give you peace
I the Lord will smile upon you and give you peace
I the Lord will be your Father, Savior, and Brother
Go my children, I will keep you and give you peace.
Go my children, sins forgiven, at peace and pure
Here you learned how much I loved you, what I can cure.

Here you learned my dear Son's story, here you touched Him, saw His glory.

Go my children, sins forgiven, at peace and pure.

Go my children, fed and nourished, closer to Me.

Grow in love by serving, joyful and free.

Here my Spirit's power filled you, here His tender comfort stilled you.

Go my children, fed and nourished, joyful and free.

Author: Jaraslov J. Vajda 1919-2008

Cassie and Jay asked me if I would do this for their future wedding, and of course, I obliged.

> Here's the story I didn't tell at the wedding: Did you hear about the couple that had more children than the Old Woman Who Lived in a Shoe? They lived so near a railroad track that they were awakened every morning at two o'clock when a freight train rumbled through, shaking the house and rattling the windows and dishes.
>
> Finally, the train would be gone and all would be completely quiet. Henry would say to his hearing impaired wife, "Do you want to go back to sleep or what?"
>
> She always answered, "What?"

CHAPTER 2

Neenah

I was born at 8:08 a.m. on March 27, as previously mentioned, at Theda Clark Hospital in Neenah, Wisconsin. Neenah is in the heart of the Fox River Valley, where papermaking is the prominent industry. Neenah is situated on the west shore of Lake Winnebago. The Fox River flows from Lake Winnebago north to Green Bay, where it empties into the Bay of Green Bay. Green Bay is the northern edge of the Fox River Valley and, going in a southerly direction, we have Kaukauna, Kimberly, Little Chute, Appleton, Grand Chute, the twin cities of Neenah and Menasha, Oshkosh, and Fond du Lac at the southern tip of Lake Winnebago.

Neenah had the highest per capita income in the United States—but of course, that was only the average, as there were extremely wealthy along with the very poor. Some were on relief, and others worked for the city, which at that time was considered next to being on relief. This was during the depth of the Great Depression, when the average wage was around thirty-five cents per hour. A loaf of bread cost five cents, as I recall.

Lake Winnebago is the largest freshwater inland lake in the United States. The lake is about forty miles long and twelve miles wide but very shallow and subject to sudden violent storms, as I know from experience. It is very popular for perch and walleye fishing, sailing, ice boating, and sturgeon spearing. There are a number of species of sturgeon, those in Russia and China reaching up to twenty-five feet in length and three thousand pounds.

The sturgeon-spearing season for Lake Winnebago runs only about sixteen days unless the limits are reached sooner. Roughly, the limits are 450 for immature females, 950 for adult females, and 1,200 for males. Here, the prehistoric-looking fish can be thirty to two hundred pounds, thirty to eighty-five inches long, and a great struggle to land once speared. Not a few shanties have been destroyed by the ordeal. The fish live to be 55 to 150 years old.

Lake Winnebago is peppered from one end to the other with these shanties, which are usually built on skids, and some are much more than mere shanties. A large hole is cut into the ice inside the shanty, and the fishermen wait, spear poised, for a target to swim into view.

The Department of Natural Resources currently issues about 12,000 licenses each season, with about 10 percent of the holders having success on average. Sturgeon caviar can be very expensive, more than gold, depending on the source and grade. If $14,000 a pound sounds expensive, compare that to the most expensive at $40,000 for a spoonful of dehydrated albino sturgeon. Beluga caviar is generally of the highest quality and most expensive. For that reason, caviar is usually sold by the gram, there being roughly 450 grams to a pound.

Neenah-Menasha was divided by Nicolet Boulevard, with Neenah on the south side and Menasha on the north. Menasha is a largely Polish and Catholic community. St. Patrick church and school was located at Nicolet and Commercial, with the Episcopal church opposite on Commercial Street. St. John's and St. Mary's were the other Catholic churches.

The Catholic church in Neenah was St. Margaret Mary, where

I would be married. Trinity Lutheran was my favorite of the Lutheran churches in Menasha. Lutheran was probably the largest denomination in Neenah, but there also were Presbyterians, Methodists, and United Brethren.

> The Hurleys, Evan and Edith, moved into a community where there was no Catholic school, so their little daughter, Susan, was going to be attending a public school. As she was leaving for school, her mother reminded her that she should be sure to find a nice Catholic girl for a friend.
>
> After a few days, Edith asked Susan if she had made friends with anyone yet and Susan said, "Oh, yes, Mommy, and I just love her. She's so sweet, we have so much fun, and we share our lunches."
>
> "And she's Catholic?" queried her mother.
>
> Susan hesitated before answering, "Well, no, but she's Metholic."

* * *

The major papermakers in Neenah were Badger Globe, Bergstrom Paper, Neenah Paper, and Kimberly-Clark, the inventor of Kleenex. Those in Menasha were Edgewater Paper, Gilbert Paper (maker of the rag paper our money is printed on), Marathon Corporation, Whiting Paper, and Wisconsin Tissue Mills. There are many related businesses, especially in Neenah, such as paper converting and printing. Some of the prominent names of the wealthy included Bergstrom, Brown, Shattuck, Kimberly, Clark, Picard, and Ward, the latter two being bankers.

The first house I remember living in was on Tyler Street, and my bedroom was off the kitchen. A woman named Germaine lived across from us, and she had red flowers, probably geraniums, on her porch. There was a store up the street, and the Art Larsens lived next to it. Our lives would meet again in the future.

We had a house fire and moved to Adams Street, which I remember only because there was a picture of me sitting on a stool outside and drinking a glass of beer. I only liked the foam then when I was three or four years old. Our next house was on Water Street. What I remember there is that there was a park behind us and a river beyond it.

At this time, I was an inveterate thumb sucker, to the point where I actually had a callous on it. My parents tried everything to break me of the habit. They put pepper and mustard on it to discourage me, but I'd suck that stuff off and keep on going.

We didn't live on Water Street very long before we moved to Gruenwald Avenue, and that was on the outskirts, perhaps even out of the city. That house had a big front porch with windows all around. My parents made sauerkraut in a big earthenware vessel, and they also made root beer, which was so good. But they never made it after that.

Joe Moocha and family were our next-door neighbors, and they had two children, Margaret and a son whose name I can't recall. He was somewhat slow and died from a fall while working on a construction job at Spring Road School. I remember Margaret because she was so beautiful. Why else would I remember her when I was that young? She would reappear later in life when she married an in-law's brother.

Joe made turtle soup and said turtles had seven kinds of meat. A girl I played with lived next to the Moochas, and she always got in trouble with her mother because when it was her turn to do the dishes, she'd put them under the sink instead of washing them.

The Christiansens were the other family I remember, because they had a new car and a son, Kenneth, who would attend the same parochial school I did. He wanted to become a minister and left for the prep school after the eighth grade. I don't know if he made it to the seminary and got ordained. Studying Greek, Latin, and German took its toll.

I don't know why we moved so often to this point, but that finally ended when we moved to Oak Street, which was home for the rest of my single life. I had an older sister and brother at the time, and two more sisters completed our family soon after. There'd be quite a surprise some years later.

Our house was one block from Wisconsin Avenue, where many of the wealthy families lived. Marshall and Charlotte Smith, a handsome couple, lived on the corner next to us. They had three children—Sandra, Howard, and Susan—all good-looking. Unfortunately, Howard had cerebral palsy.

Mr. Smith was the corporate lawyer for Kimberly Clark. My first job was with the Smiths: I mowed the lawn, raked leaves, and shoveled snow, for which I got twenty-five cents each time. The Williamses, who we never saw, were to the west of the Smiths. Next came the Masonic Temple, a couple of residences, and a small professional building where our family doctor, Fred Smith, practiced. A dentist occupied the other half of the structure.

There were two more houses on the block before the railroad tracks, and the business district started from there on. The Neenah Library stood across the street on the banks of the Fox River and adjacent to Shattuck Park, with a pavilion and a small lagoon.

Maurice DuBois and his wife lived on the opposite corner from the Smiths. They had a son who caused them great concern because he didn't start speaking until he was seven years old.

Maurice was the head chemist at Kimberly-Clark, and my lasting image is of him constantly watering his lawn. It didn't appear that the Smiths and DuBoises socialized.

Going eastward, we had the Madsens, our landlords, to whom I delivered our fifteen dollar monthly rent; the Sawtells, with beautiful Sue, who my brother had a crush on; the Jersilds, proprietors of Jersild Knitting, with ski sweaters the most popular creation; the Moultons, who were two old maid sisters in a grey stucco house with a large flower bed that provided subjects for their watercolors. Next came the Oliver Thomsens (I don't remember Mrs. Thomsen's name, but she and Mrs. Jersild were sisters; Effie was the maid), and theirs was a big, brown, comfortable place with a red-colored asphalt driveway leading to a large garage set back on the property. They had two sons, Tom and Peter, until Paul came along.

The Thomsens belonged to the Danish Lutheran Church, which eventually became part of the Evangelical Lutheran Church of America (ELCA). Tom and I were best buddies and did everything together, so I'll have more about him later.

Neenah's mayor, Edward Kalfahs, lived next door. From there on, the mansions kept getting bigger and bigger all the way to the end of Wisconsin Avenue. Now we've arrived at the drive that runs along the lakeshore, with bigger mansions set way back, to the Point (favorite make-out site), where the lighthouse stands. It ends at Riverside Park and the yacht basin filled with sailboats of all classes.

Our place on Oak Street was a two-family dwelling with a wide porch along the front and north side. Joe and Edna Jarvey occupied the front unit, which had a living room, dining room, and kitchen on the first floor. Bedrooms were upstairs. Joe was often seen stumbling home from work after a stop at his favorite watering hole. Edna had a large goiter on her throat. Emily was the older of the two daughters and was not very feminine, although she did eventually marry Bud Grant. They never had children. Joyce was taller and darker, and she became Aunt Joyce after she married my mother's fourth-youngest brother, Edwin. The girls wore boy's jockey underwear. We knew because their wash lines were in our backyard.

Our unit had a living room, a very large dining room, a small kitchen, a master bedroom, and a bathroom on the first floor. Three bedrooms and two large walk-in closets were upstairs. The stairway could be accessed from the living or dining room. Two coal-burning stoves provided the heat; there was no furnace and no hot water tank until later on. A large kettle of water was heated on the kitchen gas stove and carried to the bathtub, where enough cold water was added to reach a comfortable temperature.

The walls were papered and became smoked up in time. We cleaned them with a Play-Doh-like composition that erased the dirt remarkably well.

> Two dogs, Rusty and Fifi, a French poodle, went on their first date. When Rusty took Fifi home, he didn't know if he should shake her paw or sniff her good night.

CHAPTER 3

School Days

Trinity Lutheran church and school were located three short blocks up the street from our house. The school was a four-room structure with the gymnasium at the rear of the building and a hall beneath that. The school cafeteria was located at that level, as were the restrooms. Congregational voter meetings, rummage sales, receptions, and special dinners were held in the hall, where the dartball league also met.

I can still smell the wonderful aroma, often vegetable soup, from the kitchen that served school lunches weekdays for a price. I guess we couldn't afford that with four of us kids in school at the same time, but that didn't matter, because we lived so close to the school and could easily walk home. Enrollment at school was about 240 students, with two classes sitting side by side in each room, except the first and second grades also housed the kindergarten class, which was usually smaller than the other grades.

Starting Out

Miss Tarras taught kindergarten, first, and second grades on the first floor. She was dark, tall, and very thin, and she had an older boyfriend who stopped to see her every day in the late afternoon as he returned from work. He carried a lunch bucket, so he likely was a shift worker in a factory. She would step out into the hall with him for a few minutes, but those meetings ended after their marriage.

I didn't start school until the first grade, and I sat next to the kindergartners. Our classwork was often done from workbooks with exercises in them, and we did a lot of projects with construction paper.

Myron, a new boy, joined the kindergartners after the first week. He was a bigger lad and must have been older. He was extremely shy, wore bib overalls and just sat without any expression. It wouldn't be long before there was a pool under his chair. His parents took him out of school after the first week.

Besides Miss Tarras's extracurricular activity, I have three distinct memories from the second grade: Lowell Krenger, phonics class, and Jane Aldinger.

Lowell was slightly built and a natural comedian who often caused a disturbance. Unruly or misbehaving students were disciplined by having to go stand out in the hall for a given time sentence. Lowell would not go without a struggle. Miss Tarras would try to pull him out from his desk, but he would hook his feet around the desk, which was screwed down. As hard as she tried, she couldn't manage to remove him, so she would go across the hall and ask Mr. Stoekli for his help. Lowell had an older brother in the navy who, sadly, was washed overboard off the coast of Alaska. Lowell's family moved out of the area, so I lost a classmate. I was shocked when I heard years later that our class comedian had become an undertaker.

Phonics is a system to teach how to read and pronounce letters and sounds of letter groupings. How else would one learn how to say pronounce *psy*, *phy*, and other unnatural groupings of letters that don't have a vowel in a syllable? There was an oversized tablet on an easel stand so the pages could be flipped over to another set of the varied combinations.

Jane Aldinger was the target of my first crush, but I wasn't the only one smitten. She had long Shirley Temple curls and always wore a ribbon tied with a little bow on top of her head.

Moving Up

Miss Florence Witte taught the third and fourth grade students, and her classroom was on the second floor. She was from Sheboygan, Wisconsin, which didn't mean anything to me at the time. I wasn't sure where it was located, but I would find out in time, as I moved there after a job change and spent most of my working career there.

Miss Witte was the most meticulous person in her dress and appearance. She wore tailored, suits and her hair was always perfectly coiffed. Also, she was most precise and exact in her teaching, paying great attention to detail. She's my all-time favorite teacher, and I owe her for instilling in me the importance of education and inspiring me to be the best student possible.

Around this time, I was coming down the stairs one day when I met my older cousin, Hubert, as he was going up. I called out to him, "Hey, Hubert. Look, I have a new pair of shoes."

He looked down at them and said, "Well, isn't that nice," and promptly stomped on my right shoe, crushing the toe. Nevertheless, years later, I would be the best man at his wedding.

It was back to the first floor for the fifth and sixth grades, taught by Mr. Winfred Stoekli—again, a very strict teacher who demanded your attention. He wasn't averse to whipping an eraser at an idling student, and he was quite accurate. Blackboards were a common teaching tool.

Sharing a classroom had an advantage in that you could take in the instruction of the higher grade when not busy with your own classwork, so it was like getting a double education. I mostly remember his math classes and then drawing, in part because I learned how to draw three-dimensional objects.

Grades 7 and 8

Mr. William Hellerman, Wild Bill, was our seventh- and eighth-grade teacher. He also was the school principal, choir director, and church organist. Our classroom was on the fourth floor until half the gymnasium was partitioned off to provide more classroom space.

Mr. Hellerman always had a crew cut, wore high-top shoes, and walked like a duck as he wobbled from side to side with his head bobbing. He was German though and through, got his nickname because of his quick temper, and had a ruler in his arsenal. He was strictly a no-nonsense character. He, like Miss Witte, was a perfectionist when it came to teaching. He lived across the intersection from the school and never owned a car. He taught until he was eighty years old.

Each classroom displayed a church flag and an American flag. Our school day began with a prayer and the Pledge of Allegiance to the flag. Honesty, loyalty, and patriotism were stressed. The curriculum included all the usual subjects like mathematics, American history, and geography, but there also was Bible history, art and music appreciation, and singing.

Trinity was known to the public school kids as the Dutch College. We did a lot of singing in harmony, and the music carried throughout the school. We sang at funerals, as the school was adjacent to the church, and we were always practicing cantatas, either for a religious observance such as Easter or for a patriotic holiday like Washington's birthday. That composition included a plea sung in a hymn-like manner that I'll always remember:

Traveler when you pass that way

Will you not in silence pray

That our land may ever be

Worthy of its history.

By a thousand memories bound,

Valley Forge is solemn ground.

Another segment of the composition had to do with Washington and the creation of the first American flag. I'm sorry I can't recall it in its entirety, but it went like this:

Mistress Betsy Ross they say

In her Arch Street home one day

Saw proceeding down the street

Callers, one, two, three.

Mistress Betsy Ross said they

In her Arch Street home that day

Will you.......????????

Author: Unknown

I was an eighth-grader when Mr. Hellerman called to me up front one day after our singing session ended and said, "Someday, you are going to be making a living with your voice." I won't hold you in suspense, as that never happened. We were a poor family, and at that time, I didn't have any hopes of going on to school, whether to study music or anything else.

Another memory about Mr. Hellerman is that he kicked me out of church—twice, in fact. I always sat in the balcony, which had wooden seats, not pews. One day a few seconds before the bells were going to ring for the start of church, an old geezer blew his nose. It was so loud, it broke the complete silence and sounded like one of those horns with a big rubber bulb: *HOOONK, HOOONK*. I couldn't control my laughter and was asked to leave. The other time I was creating a distraction because the belt buckle from my coat was rattling around in my seat.

It was the start of a new school year, and a Mrs. Prussy was going to be the new teacher. She introduced herself and added, "When we come back to class tomorrow, I want you to tell me my name."

She explained how important it was to address people by their proper name, as that would impress people who would in turn remember you. She went on, "The best way to remember something is to create a mental image of it. Now, my name is Mrs. Prussy. That's pussy with an 'r' in it."

Naturally, the next day, only little Johnny raised his hand when she asked the class who could remember her name.

"Wonderful, Johnny, and would you please tell the class what my name is?"

"Yeah," said Johnny. "It's Mrs. Crunt."

Miss Woodson was a dedicated grade-school teacher and understood a high percentage of learning is achieved in one's early years She realized it was important for children to build a good vocabulary and tried to impress this upon the students. It was important to her, too, in the interest of her students, so she initiated a program to encourage the children to apply themselves. The idea was to give them a weekly assignment to use the given word in a personal experience and report it to the class.

The program was working well until the fourth week, when the assignment was a more difficult word, *contagious*. When it seemed no student had an answer, Miss Woodson was delighted to see Johnny getting to his feet.

"Now, Johnny, please tell the class about your experience."

Johnny told them he was riding around with his father when they passed a woman on a ladder and his dad said, "It's going to take that *contageous* to paint the house with that brush."

CHAPTER 4

Playmates

Tom Thomsen was the only boy my age who lived in the neighborhood, so I spent a great deal of time with my three sisters and a couple of girls when Tom wasn't around. We played hopscotch, jacks, and pick-up sticks. We jumped rope and roller-skated. The shoe skates were an adjustable platform on metal wheels, so the length could be adjusted according to the size of your shoes. The skate, strapped around the ankle, clamped onto your shoe soles. A key, usually hanging around the neck, was used to adjust the clamps. It was a problem if your soles were too worn.

The idea in hopscotch was to do the course as fast as possible. We didn't have real skip ropes but used lengths of clothesline. It was hop, hop, both feet, left foot, right foot, double skip, crisscross, and do the whole thing backward. I realized in time that I developed balance, coordination, and agility with these activities. If I were an athletic coach, these would be part of my training program, as would distance running to build endurance.

Tom and I had a jungle call, "Aaah yurrr aah!" (forget Tarzan). There were few days, especially in summer months, when we didn't get together.

Tom had large buck teeth, and I went with him to his dentist every Saturday morning to have his braces adjusted. The teeth were being drawn back by catgut instead of wires, and the dentist, Dr. Schultz, would actually lift Tom out of the chair as he strained to tighten the setup. I don't know if Tom had any discomfort during the process, as he never complained.

It was on a winter morning when, after two years, the braces came off. I wasn't with him that morning, nor was I with him when he went ice-skating that afternoon, fell, and broke his front teeth off at the gumline.

He was skating at Columbian Park, more commonly referred to as the Green. The Green was not a large park; it occupied about two thirds of a block. In winter, it became a huge skating rink as the city flooded it and kept it plowed so that there was a snowbank ten to twelve feet high encircling the ice. The rink was illuminated at night and would be crowded with skaters. There was a brick warming house with the inner walls lined with benches. The park was just two short blocks from where I lived, so I spent a lot of time there.

In the milder weather, most of the activities centered around baseball and the two tennis courts. One corner of the park was devoted to the usual park amenities: swings, trapeze bar, monkey bars, slide, and sandbox. Tom and I swung on the trapeze bar a lot. We took turns swinging as high as possible and then letting go to see which of us could jump the farthest. Our schoolyard wasn't large enough for us to play ball, so we went to the park during recess periods, as it was located just one half block away.

Apparently, Tom wasn't doing well in his mathematics class, and his mother asked me if I could help him. I explained the decimal system and had him do simple adding and subtraction problems before going into multiplication table drills.

We played inside during inclement weather, but I didn't mind that at all, because the playroom was so well stocked with toys, games, and stuffed animals. Tom had a better imagination than I did. Once in a while, I'd be invited to stay for lunch, and peanut butter or egg salad sandwiches were common fare.

The Thomsens went on vacation to Mexico and came home with a Chihuahua puppy they named Popo after visiting Mount Popocatepetl, an active volcano. When they came home from a Canadian vacation, Tom's face was all scarred up. He dove into six inches of water that looked much deeper because it was so crystal clear. He could have broken his neck.

Tom and I saw less and less of each other in the following years, as we both made other friends through school and associations. Gordy, Red, and Whitey were the schoolmates I liked, and Tom became friends with Dick Baer, who I didn't care to be around.

Gordy Payne was left-handed and had two brothers and a sister. All the boys were interested in building model airplanes from kits and were very good at it. The kits were of balsa wood and formed the skeleton of the planes, while the skin was made from tissue paper, which was fitted and glued on. The tissue paper became perfectly taut when it dried after misting it with water. Model airplane building required a lot of patience. Gordy became at auditor for the state of Wisconsin. Unfortunately, he died when he was about forty.

Jerald "Whitey" Kuckenbecker, another classmate, and I had great fun together. He lived in a nice new home built by his father, who was in the home-construction business with a brother. Whitey's sister, Jean, never missed a day of school all through grade school and high school. She was also a straight-A student.

Whitey's mother was nothing but sweet, and she worked in a downtown dress shop. Whitey and I washed the store widows there every Saturday morning. He was very close to his mother and had a very difficult time when she died of cancer. I thought Whitey and I would stay best friends forever, but we drifted apart over time as we developed different interests.

Earl "Red" Page and I were the best baseball players in grade school. Both of us were good hitters and competed for the longest home runs. Red was bigger than me, so I had the edge there. We played basketball, beat the public school team, and became co-captains of our high school team.

Red was a natural artist. His drawings of deer and horses were especially amazing. I loved to watch him draw, as he made it look so easy. I liked to draw too, but I didn't have the natural talent he possessed.

Red's family moved to a location several houses away from the Green. He had a younger sister, Carol, who came screaming home from playing at the park. She was terrified that she was going to die. Gladys had never told her daughter that she would someday become a young woman.

Red's father was the chauffer for the Shattuck family. The Shattuck mansion sat on the river's edge. The Pilgrim, a huge ocean-going cruise ship, was anchored there. The Shattucks had another pleasure boat, a Chris Craft, and Red's father took the two of us out on a Sunday excursion on Lake Winnebago. His father's knowledge of the lake saved our lives day.

It was a beautiful, warm, sunny afternoon, and we were speeding over the calm water when Red's dad spotted a sudden squall coming up on the near horizon. He immediately headed, full bore, straight to the nearest shore. By the time we reached the shore, only minutes later, the storm was upon us, and the lake was a tempest.

A man on shore saw us heading in and came out to offer help. By that time, the waters were so rough they were unable to secure the boat. Each man held on to the boat with one hand and the dock with the other as the boat heaved up and down with the waves. The Chris Craft would have been smashed to pieces on the rocks without the man's help. Each year, there are a number of drownings on the lake, and we could have been victims ourselves.

> Nancy had her hand inside Sluggo's pants and said, "No wonder boys can run faster than girls: ball bearings and a stick shift!"

CHAPTER 5

Childhood Memories

Going off on a tangent, the following are some random memories from my childhood:

❖ Each spring, my dad would have all of us kids line up for his magical elixir: sulfur and molasses to purify our blood.

❖ Dad was the family gardener and usually planted carrots, green beans, and tomato plants. Ox Heart was his favorite variety of tomato, and the plants produced big, solid tomatoes. The plants must have thrived on the eggshells, coffee grounds, and fish guts Dad worked into the soil as fertilizers.

❖ Knickers and knee socks were popular attire for young boys. The elastic in the knickers would wear out, as would the elastic in the knee socks, so both would fall down. I'd pull the socks and knickers up and hold them in place with a rubber band. Knickers were often made of corduroy and would make a *whip, whip* sound as you walked until the ribs wore down.

❖ When the collars of our shirts wore out, my mother would take them off and reverse them so the shirts were like new again.

❖ Dad was a hunter and fisherman. I liked going with him, as he was an expert marksman and rarely missed the squirrel or rabbit he took aim at. Mom's fried squirrel and rabbit were a treat. I also liked inland fishing in summer but hated ice fishing, because I just froze standing around. At times, Dad would lie on the ice and peer into the hole as he jigged the bait, which often was chicken neck skin.

❖ Three of my mother's brothers—Rudolph, Karl, and Edward, in that order—lived with us as they came off the farm to look for employment. Jobs were pretty scarce, but Dad got Rudy and Karl into the paper mill, where he was a beater engineer. Each one stayed until he got married, which didn't seem to take long. Rudy, who always raided the icebox, married and got divorced after three children. He would be killed by a hit-and-run driver. Uncle Eddie married Joyce, one of the girls living next door. She once treated us kids to Ritz crackers and ginger ale. Uncle Karl was my favorite. He had a car, took me to the zoo, and bought me an ice cream cone.

❖ I had frequent ear aches I'd like to forget.

Childhood Diseases

German measles, mumps, chicken pox, and scarlet fever were common communicable childhood diseases when I was a boy. Of course, polio was feared, as the Sauk vaccine had not yet been invented. Measles was probably the most common and least serious. I believe mumps could cause sterility for adult victims.

I don't remember that we were quarantined for chicken pox, but we were for scarlet fever. Scarlet fever was announced by a sign on red paper that was nailed to the door, and no visitors were allowed. Even my father could not come into his own house, so he lived with his sister during the quarantine period, which I believe lasted two weeks. He stopped by every day on his way home from work but had to stay outside.

It was during these times that I learned a little about home economics, as I observed my mother cooking, baking, cleaning, doing the washing and ironing, sewing, knitting, darning socks, etc. When she made an apple pie, I was right there to eat the apple peelings, usually one big long strip per apple. I was right there to lick the spoon when she made a cake and made sure I was around to get the heel of a warm loaf of bread.

Sometimes my mother fried bread, and I loved that. It was kind of a homemade version of an English muffin, with butter and honey or maple syrup.

I learned to knit, probably because there was nothing else to do. I started with a scarf and then made a pair of mittens before tackling argyle socks. I never knitted after that, but I found out later it isn't that uncommon for older men to wield the needles.

Brownie

Brownie was the real joy of my early childhood. He was my best friend, companion and consolation. He loved me as much as I loved him.

I was spending some vacation time at Uncle Richard's farm in Fremont when I was about ten years old. Uncle Richard, my mother's oldest brother, and Aunt Viola had one child, Dick, who was just three months younger than I was. Their dog had recently had a litter of pups, and I had my pick. Brownie was a collie and shepherd mix. He could have passed for a collie, but he didn't have the long nose. Just a handsome dog.

I entered him in the annual pet and hobby show and got him ready by taking him to the lake for a bath. He won the All American Breed trophy by being his beautiful self. He also won the obedience trophy, for which I had to have him sit in the middle of the arena while I walked around outside of it. He never moved, except his head turned and eyes followed me as I walked around. He didn't move until I gave him the command, "Come."

One Friday night, I had a telephone call from my oldest sister, who was working at the Woolworth 5 & 10 store. Somehow, our Aunt Mandy had witnessed a commotion and thought it involved our dog. It seemed Brownie had slipped out of his collar and followed my sister when she went to work, just two blocks from home. The Northwestern 400 Streamliner was coming, and she had crossed the tracks, but Brownie was hit as he tried to beat it. I got there just as a police officer pulled out his pistol and shot Brownie in the head as he was lying right in front of me. The cop was a brother of my future father-in-law. Somehow, a brief report appeared in the local newspaper, and it stated that I was inconsolable.

Did you hear about the cross-eyed seamstress?
She couldn't "mend straight."

Blank's Grocery Store

Every neighborhood had a grocery store, and ours was just a couple of blocks away, across from our church and school. Two brothers, Gus and Sweeny, were the proprietors. All fresh vegetables were at the front of the store, and the meat counter was along the back wall. The checkout counter was on one side, and a candy counter was opposite.

We had an account there, and I was sent to pay the bill every week. In appreciation, I guess, Gus would give us a pint of ice cream, and we all got a slice of it. Blanks also delivered groceries, and Sweeny was the grocery man.

One day, as I was walking past the store, I saw my reflection in the window. I walked with my head tilted back and bobbed up and down. I must have been rocking up on the balls of my feet. From then on, I made a conscious effort to keep my chin down and took the lift out of my walk. There was another problem, but I didn't realize it until I got into high school.

In addition to having a grocery man, in those days we had a milkman, an iceman, a coal man, an insurance man, a Watkins man, a Fuller Brush man, and of course, the mailman. Refrigeration was provided by an icebox, so it was necessary to have an iceman. He came every week, brought the forty-pound blocks of ice into the house, and loaded them into the upper level.

Coal was sold by the ton, and customers had a choice of soft or bituminous coal. The coal man would pull up alongside a house and put a coal chute through a basement window to fill the coal bin. By the end of the day, he'd be as black as the coal itself.

Mr. Martin was our milkman and was the nicest man. He reminded me of my Uncle Karl. Mr. Martin took me on his milk route one day, and I helped him deliver. The truck had open sides so it was easy to hop in and out.

I had only indirect contact with the mailman, but I know he

remembered me. Shortly after I started driving, when I backed out of our driveway. I thought I was up against the curbing, so I gave it a little more gas and tore up the side of his brand new car, which he had parked opposite from our driveway.

Little Annie's father traveled most of the week, so he'd take her driving on the weekends so they had some time together for bonding. She loved it. When he was too under the weather one week to take her, he saw how disappointed she was, so he suggested her mommy take her. When they returned, Annie excitedly raced up to her daddy and said, "Guess what, Daddy. We didn't see one asshole, dirty bastard, or son of a bitch!"

Tennis

My oldest sister, Gert, was four years older than I was, and I owe her for getting me interested in competitive sports. Initially, she got me into tennis when I was in the eighth grade. I had a natural backhand stroke, and my ball would hop cross court. My forehand was weak, so I would run around it when possible.

By forcing myself to play forehand shots, I developed a very strong stroke and hit hard, deep balls. However, my backhand suffered as a consequence and became a weakness in my game until I redeveloped it years later after many matches with superior players I met and became friends with through tennis tournaments.

It was when Gert took me to a high school basketball game that I saw a world of sports I didn't know existed and wanted to be a part of. I'll come back to this later.

Boys' Brigade

The Boys' Brigade was founded in Glasgow by Sir William Alexander Smith in 1883 to develop Christian manliness by use of a semi-military discipline and order, gymnastics, summer camps and religious services. I learned of the organization from my friend, Red Page, and we both joined.

The local facility is in downtown Neenah and includes a gymnasium. The rear of the property abuts the Presbyterian Church, of recent construction, large and beautiful with attractive grounds. Most of the Brigade leaders were members there. I distinctly remember two of them, Warren Whitlinger and Jerry Verstegen, as they treated us like young gentlemen. It was apparent they were great friends. Many years later, a Whitlinger girl became the state tennis champion, and she is likely his granddaughter.

I must add an insert here after I learned more about this wonderful man. He was only five feet nine and 170 pounds, but he went to Ohio State University on scholarship and led the league in scoring. He earned a master's degree and played professional basketball. All three of his children—John, Tami, and Teri—went to Stanford and became professional tennis players. Whit died in 2012 at the age of ninety-eight. Rest in peace, Mr. Whitlinger.

Red and I played in the basketball league, and that gave me an introduction to coaching and organized play that I hadn't experienced previously. The semi-military aspects included drilling (left face, right face, about face, right oblique). Marching and rifle drills taught us how to shoulder a weapon and follow commands, like "Present arms."

This experience must have been evident when I reported for ROTC training in college, as the leader, Major Bozeman, quickly singled me out and made me the company commander. That put me at the head of my unit as we marched in local parades.

The Brigade own Camp Onaway, six acres set in the idyllic Chain O' Lakes in Waupaca, Wisconsin. The twenty-two connected lakes are spring-fed, deep, clear blue, and favored for any water-related activity such as fishing or kayaking, to name a couple. Lake cruises were very popular and ran from a number of locations. I recall Edmund's Boat Dock, our launching site to head to the island, and Ding's Dock. Cruise vessels came in all sizes, including a sixty-foot paddle-wheeler.

There are two significant facilities located on the Chain I should mention: Indian Crossing Casino, for dancing and entertainment (but not gambling), and the Wisconsin Veteran's Home, situated on a four-hundred-acre site and built before the turn of the nineteenth century for the care of indigent honorably discharged soldiers, sailors, or Marines, and for indigent wives or widows.

Nothing could have exceeded the excitement I experienced as I anticipated what would become my first camping endeavor as a twelve year old, but something happened to take much of the joy out of it. The day after arriving, I found my hands had become severely swollen, and I reported to headquarters to see a counselor. I had an infection under the calluses developed from swinging on the trapeze at the Green with Tom.

Two leaders took me to a doctor in Waupaca. He froze the palms of my hands and made incisions from the little fingers and middle fingers to the center of my palms. The fluids spurted up like little geysers. My hands were bandaged, and that precluded me from participating in a lot of events. The leaders must have paid the doctor out of their own pockets. Good guys!

Bandaged hands didn't prevent me from attending chapel or

the campfires. Each night, a different leader led chapel, and each kept the campers' full attention with such inspirational messages that one looked forward to the next time. Chapel always closed with a familiar hymn.

What do you do around campfires? You sing! Solomon Levi was a Jewish tailor, and the following is the 1930 newspaper advertisement he hoped would help his business:

> My name is Solomon Levi,
> And my store's on Salem Street;
> That's where to buy your coats and vests
> And everything else that's neat;
> Second-handed ulsterettes
> And overcoats so fine.
> For all the boys that trade with me
> At Hundred and Forty-nine.
> *Published 1885 by Ditson, Oliver & Co.*

I recall our singing only the first two stanzas of the next song, but I found the additional verses:

Johnny Verbeck
There was a little Dutch boy, his
name was Johnny Verbeck.
He was a dealer in sausages and
sauerkraut and spec.
He made the finest sausages you
ever would have seen.
One day he invented the
sausage-making machine.
Oh, Mr. Johnny Verbeck, how
could you be so mean?

I told you you'd be sorry for in-
venting that machine.
Now all the neighbors' cats and
dogs will never more be seen.
They've all been ground to sausages
in Johnny Verbeck's machine.
Author: Al Tanous, 1926–1990

Again, there are more verses to the next song than we sang, so
I've excluded them, as I think they distract from the main thrust.
To me, the song seems complete without them:

My Grandfather's Clock
My grandfather's clock was
too large for the shelf,
So it stood ninety years on the floor.
It was taller by half than the old man himself,
Though it weighed not a pennyweight more.
It was bought on the morn of
the day that he was born
And was always his treasure and pride.
But it stopped short, never to go again,
When the old man died.
Ninety years without slumber-
ing ... *tick, tock, tick, tock.*
His life's seconds number-
ing ... *tick, tock, tick, tock.*
But it stopped short, never to go again,
When the old man died.
In watching its pendulum swing to and fro
Many hours had he spent while a boy,
And in childhood and manhood
the clock seemed to know

And to share both his grief and his joy.
Ninety years without slumbering …
Written in 1876 by Henry Clay Work

Reggie and Sapphire, newlyweds, were undressing in preparation for their first marital encounter. When Reggie removed his shoes and stockings, Sapphire noticed his toes were quite shriveled.

"Reggie, honey, whatever happened to your toes?"

"Oh, I had toemain poisoning when I was young."

When he dropped his trousers, Sapphire noticed with dismay, "Reggie, what happened to your knees?"

"Oh," replied Reggie, "I had kneemonia when I was young."

Moments later Sapphire gushed relief. "Oh, Reggie, thank goodness, I was so afraid you might have had dicktheria, too!"

Summers on the Farm

I usually spent my boyhood summers at Uncle Richard's. Cousin Dick and I were just three months apart in age. I well remember one summer at Uncle Jack's in Bear Creek. That is near Sugar Bush, where I was picked up at the train station, having taken the milk train from Neenah. Sugar Bush had a feed mill and a pickle factory. You'll never find more contented cows than those who are fed ground wheat and silage.

I always thought Uncle Jack was my dad's stepbrother because he was a Thomack too, but my sister said they were cousins. I asked why we called him "Uncle Jack," and she said, "It's because he married Aunt Alma." Aunt Alma and our mother were sisters. Jack and Alma had two children, Wesley and Gladys, four years and two years older than I was.

I had my first driving experience there one day when Wes and I were out in the potato field knocking potato bugs off the plants with a cedar shingle. We'd catch the bugs in a five-gallon pail. It was a very hot and humid day, and Wes told me to take the car, a Model T Ford, to go fetch more cold coffee from the house. I told him I had never driven, but he assured me I'd do just fine, and away I went.

There was a deep ditch running alongside the road with a culvert by the farm entrance, and I was really going too fast to make the turn. I careened over the ditch and nearly struck one of the poplar trees lining the driveway. Aunt Alma happened to be looking out and saw me coming. Her jaw dropped and her eyes grew wide open, probably wider than mine. Somehow, I managed to brake just short of the pigsty.

Aunt Alma canned meats, beef, and venison in two-quart Mason jars. I didn't care much for the beef, but it was better than the venison, which was just awful-tasting to me. There was a cedar swamp on the farm property, and that was where Uncle Jack hunted the deer, so it may have affected the flavor. I don't know what spice Aunt Alma added, but it may have been bay leaf, which I still don't care for. Years later, I was given some venison chops in Kentucky, and how I loved them.

One day, I stepped on a large rusty nail that poked all the way through my foot. Uncle Jack took some tobacco he was chewing, put it on my foot, and packed cow manure on top of that to draw out any infection and to prevent blood poisoning. Did the trick!

There was a cheese factory about a mile from the farm, and Uncle Jack hauled his milk there as all the local farmers did. The cans of milk were loaded onto a big wagon pulled by King and Queen, his team of horses. Behind the factory stood an icehouse, a barnlike structure. Huge blocks of ice cut from frozen lakes were stored in the loft and packed in sawdust. It was amazing the ice never melted despite the summer heat.

Aunt Alma made ice cream, and I have yet to find any that tastes better than hers did. At times, she added freshly ripened strawberries for an added treat.

I've always loved animals of all kinds, so it really bothered me when the pigs were slaughtered. The pigs were shot in the head and their throats were slit. The blood was collected to make blood sausage (I never tried it). You can imagine what head cheese was made of.

One day Queen, from Uncle Jack's team of horses, was going to be bred, and when the stud service arrived, I was sent to the farmhouse. I was deemed too young to witness the action. I detoured and hid in the grainery to watch the goings-on. That was my introduction to animal husbandry, and I would later witness similar activity by pigs, cows, and ducks. I was fortunate to be there when Queen delivered a beautiful colt, Prince, but it lived only three days.

The pharmacist was giving a woman instructions for use of a product she was purchasing. "Apply it to your arms twice a day," he said.

But the woman cut him off. "It's not for my arms. It's for my schnauzer," she bristled.

"Oh, in that case," retorted the pharmacist, "apply it three times a day and don't take a bath for a week."

Thadeus and Bertha were driving through the hills of Kentucky when Bertha quite suddenly had need of restroom facilities. "Taddy," she cried, "you have to hurry, because I really have to get to a bathroom right now!"

"Bertha," he replied, "you know I'm driving as fast as I can. If you can't hold it, you'll just have to hang it out the window and let it fly."

She had no choice and … *SPLAAAAT!* … she plastered two hillbillies standing along the roadside waiting for the car to pass.

Clem says to Fletch, "What in tarnation whar that?"

"Danged if I know, but you see the set of jaws on that critter?"

CHAPTER 6

World War II

Countless books have been written about World II, the great battles and the war heroes along with many other aspects. While I love history and documentaries pertaining to the war, I am not a historian and am not veering off here in that direction. However, patriotism and interest in national affairs are piqued by involvement, and unification of the country is more important than at any other time.

The United States was trying to maintain neutrality but was supplying war materials to Britain in its war with Germany, which had already overrun Poland and France by 1941, so we were already indirectly involved. I was just ten years old at the time but learned of certain events of great concern as the family huddled around the radio for news of the latest developments. Franklin Delano Roosevelt, FDR, was our president and my hero.

Radio not only brought us the news but also entertainment. Music provided that entertainment as well as inspiration through patriotic songs, of which many were composed and popularized during the war. There was one song I can recall that preceded the war but I believe was important to promote a common cause.

Kate Smith was probably the most popular singer, the queen of radio, during the 1940s. Irving Berlin chose her to introduce his latest composition, "God Bless America." There were rumors and rumblings of war, and Berlin called them "storm clouds" in the preamble of the song:

> While the storm clouds gather far across the sea,
> Let us pledge allegiance to a land that's free.
> Let us all be grateful for a land so fair
> As we raise our voices in common prayer:
> God bless America, land that I love
> Stand beside her and guide her
> Through the night with a light from above.
> From the mountains to the prairies
> To the oceans white with foam
> God bless America, my home sweet home.

"The Star Spangled Banner" is our national anthem, but there is another patriotic song, "America the Beautiful," that is also very popular, and that popularity increased after 9/11. The lyrics by Katherine Lee Bates paint a glorious picture of our country and date from 1895. The music, originally for a different song, was composed by Samuel Ward, a church organist and choirmaster at Grace Episcopal Church in Newark, New Jersey. Bates penned eight stanzas to this song, but I will show just the first, which is the only one most people know, and third, which I think is very poignant.

America the Beautiful
Oh beautiful for spacious skies,
For amber waves of grain,
For purple mountain majesty
Above the fruited plain.

America! America!
God shed his grace on thee,
And crown thy good with brotherhood
From sea to shining sea.
Oh beautiful for heroes proved
In liberating strife,
Who more than self their country loved
And mercy more than life.
America! America!
May God thy gold refine,
'Til all success be nobleness
And every gain divine.

Food Stamps

The war was being fought overseas, but overtones were felt everywhere, and rationing impacted everyone. Coffee, sugar, meat, butter, cheese, rubber, shoes, and gas were rationed items. Water and the free air we breathed were about the only things that weren't.

Food-stamp books were issued to families. Quantities must somehow have been determined by the number of members in them. Stamps had expiration dates. There were red, blue, green, and brown stamp books, which covered specific items. For instance, red stamps were for meats and blue for processed and canned goods, juices, fruit, etc.

Farmers were allotted extra gasoline to operate tractors and trucks. Each farmer had a special tank for the gasoline that had a red dye in it and was unlawful to use for passenger vehicles. (Ha, ha!) The speed limit was set at thirty-five miles per hour to help lower consumption of gas. The government established the Office of Price Administration to ward off gouging, and violators of any of the rules were subject to ten years in prison, a fine of $10,000, or both.

While the population was spending stamps for rationed products, they were collecting stamps of another kind. S&H Green Stamps was a line of trading stamps by the Sperry & Hutchison company. Actually, the Green Stamp program had begun in the 1930s. Stamps were purchased from S&L by businesses and issued to their customers, who could redeem them for merchandise from S&H. Stamps could be one, ten, or fifty points. The stamp book had twenty-four pages, and it took fifty points to fill one page, so a full book represented 1,200 points.

Supermarkets, department stores and gasoline stations were typical retailers that issued the stamps as bonuses, based on the amount of the purchases, at the checkout counter. Collectors "purchased" chosen items at a local Green Stamps store or from the S&L catalog. The S&L catalog contained 40,000 premiums, and S&L's motto was "Everything for the Home."

Victory Gardens

People were encouraged to plant gardens, and chances are they did so if any suitable space was available. This is how Victory Gardens came into being, and it was a most successful program—to the degree that 40 percent of national consumption was provided by them. From the war effort standpoint, much less manpower had to be devoted to farming.

War Bonds

Another way to support the war effort (and "do your part") was to participate in the war bond program. Bonds of $25 to $1,000 were sold for 75 percent of the redemption value; i.e., $18.75 for a $25 bond. The bonds had a ten-year maturity period but could be redeemed earlier at the accumulated value. Participation was encouraged by easy methods such as payroll deduction or bond stamps, which were a popular program for younger children. Bond stamps cost ten cents, and a full book would purchase a $25 bond.

War bond sales drives were common and hugely successful, with the many of the biggest Hollywood stars going on tours. Newspapers provided a lot of publicity and helped the cause.

Media Bloopers and Other Blunders

A bakery sponsored a news show on a Minneapolis radio station. The commercial, which started, "For the best in bread …" was repeated numerous times during the hour, but the announcer read it one time too often, as he said, "For the breast in bed …" and got himself fired.

Fran Tarkington was a Minnesota Viking quarterback, and the most elusive when he was flushed out of the pocket. After retirement, he was given a shot on a national sports show during the football training camp period. A point is reached when teams have to reduce their squads to a given number, and that's when Fran announced, "Well, folks, it's nut-cutting time." He couldn't escape that one.

The Sheboygan radio station offered the public free advertising on a Saturday morning show. I was listening when the announcer said, "For sale: Hand crotched [*crocheted*] rugs. Call …"

There was a clipping from the local newspaper classified ads section pinned to the bulletin board at a tavern where I played cribbage. It read: "For sale. Three bedroom ranch, bath and a half, finished basement and extra large dick."

Repetition does not lead to perfection. Biscuit and Cracker was one of the departments in the food packaging plant I worked at. During a meeting, the manager referenced Biscuit and Cracker, Biscuit and Cracker, one time too often, and came out with "Biscuit and Crapper."

We used a lot of die-cast aluminum parts in the compressor products manufactured by Thomas Industries, where I worked during the sixties and seventies. We cast some of the parts in our own die-casting department, but two other locations in our company—Sparta, Tennessee, and Fort Atkinson, Wisconsin—supplied some as well. Certain issues kept arising until finally the plant manager decided to put an end to them once and for all. He was ranting on and on to the staff about Sparta and Fort, Sparta and Fort, when he emphatically cried, "And that's the last I want to hear about Sporta and Fart!"

Alliteration? Can you repeat "Freddy Fuddpucker, Freddy Fuddpucker, Freddy Fuddpucker" within 3 seconds? Try it.

CHAPTER 7

Confirmation

S tudents going to a parochial elementary school received religious instruction in a number of ways, but mostly through Bible study and Bible lessons until advancing to the confirmation class. Graduation culminates in church membership, which entitles participation in the Sacrament of the Altar. The only other sacrament Lutherans practice is that of Holy Baptism.

Our Bible history book contained pictures of glorious paintings depicting certain events, such as Adam and Eve in the Garden of Eden, Sampson, David and Goliath, the Nativity, Jacob's Ladder, Christ in the Garden of Gethsemane, the Crucifixion, and the Resurrection. I have vivid memories of them all.

The Ten Commandments, the Creed, the Lord's Prayer, Confession, and the Sacrament of the Altar were the general topics of instruction. Of course, Luther's Small Catechism (only small in comparison to his large, voluminous catechism) was the basis for instruction, which was the responsibility of the pastor. Our pastor, Gerhard Schaeffer, was adept at illustrating the lessons, which made them all the more interesting. Student assignments were generally to commit material to memory for recitation in subsequent classes.

The class appeared before the congregation for Examination to demonstrate understanding of the tenets of faith. The pastor possed questions for the confirmands to answer. Examination Night was usually on Maundy Thursday, commemorating the institution of the Lord's Supper (Sacrament of the Altar).

The class was dressed in white robes, and the girls wore corsages, while the boys sported carnations. The confirmation rite concluded with the class singing the hymn it chose: "I Need Thee Every Hour," "My Faith Looks Up to Thee," or another appropriate offering.

There was one thing about the communion service that I found to be very touching: Pastor Schaeffer took Communion only after all others had been served. "Feed my lambs."

Martin Luther

Martin Luther is credited with starting the parochial school system (and the tradition of Christmas trees), and he saw the need for the catechism. In his preface to the catechism, Luther states, "The deplorable, miserable conditions which I recently observed when visiting the parishes have constrained and pressed me to put this catechism of Christian doctrine into this brief, plain, and simple form. How pitiable, so help me God, were the things I saw: the common man, especially in the villages, knows nothing of Christian doctrine and unable to teach."

Luther translated the New Testament of the Bible from Greek into German so it could be read by a larger population of people. This was made possible by Gutenberg's movable-type printing press.

Not only was Luther a prolific author, he excelled in hymn writing and is credited with composing the melodies as well for some of the thirty-six hymns he wrote, including twenty-four in the first year of this endeavor. "A Mighty Fortress Is Our God" became known as the Battle Hymn of the Reformation. Said Luther:

- ❖ "Beautiful music is the art of the prophets that can calm the agitations of the soul; it is the delightful present God has given us."
- ❖ "Our Lord has written the promise of Resurrection, not in the books alone but in every leaf of springtime."
- ❖ "God writes the Gospel not in the Bible alone, but also in the trees and in the flowers and clouds and sky."
- ❖ "The first thing I ask is that people should not make the use of my name and should not call themselves Lutherans but Christians. What is Luther? The teaching is not mine. Nor was I crucified for anyone. How did I, poor stinking bag of maggots that I am, come to the point where people call the children of Christ by my evil name?"

Luther wrote hymns to convey relevant messages for the liturgical occasions of the church year: Christmas, Easter, Pentecost, Trinity, etc. They were important means for the development of faith. It is simply amazing how he was able to produce such voluminous works with only a rudimentary instrument to pen them.

In the year 1505, Luther, on the verge of becoming a lawyer, was caught in such a violent, horrific storm that he feared for his life and vowed to Saint Anna, the mother of the Virgin Mary, "Save me and I'll become a monk." He became much more than a mere monk: Dr. Martin Luther, 1483–1546.

Luther helped twelve nuns escape and found mates for all but one, Katherine von Bora. They were not in love when he married her himself, but they grew to love and cherish each other. Luther was forty-one years old when they married, and they had six children. He wrote, "There is no more lovely, friendly, and charming relationship, communion, or company than a good marriage." He was an exemplary husband and father.

Luther was a jolly person and quipped, "If there's no laughter in heaven, I don't want to go there."

He could also be quite earthy: "A happy fart never comes from a miserable ass."

Luther's Rose

Also called Luther's Seal, this is a black cross on a red heart, on a white rose, in a sky-blue field bordered by a gold ring. When Luther saw the drawing of the seal designed by Lazarus Spengler at the behest of John Frederick the Magnanimous of Saxony, he saw it as an expression of his theological faith and wrote the following to Spengler:

> First, there is a black cross that remains its natural color. This is to remind me that it is faith in the Crucified one that saves us. Anyone who believes from the heart will be justified (Romans 10:10). It is a black cross, which mortifies and causes pain, but it leaves the heart its natural color. It doesn't destroy nature, that is to say, it does not kill us but keeps us alive, for the just shall live by faith in the Crucified one (Romans 1:17). The hearts should stand in the middle of a white rose. This is to show that faith gives joy, comfort and peace—it puts the believer into a white, joyous rose. Faith does not give peace and joy like the world gives (John 14:27). This is why the rose must be white, not red. White is the color of the spirits and angels (cf. Matthew 28:3; John 20:12). The rose should

stand in a sky-blue field, symbolizing that a joyful spirit is a beginning of heavenly, future joy, which begins now, but is grasped in hope, not yet fully revealed. Around the field of blue is a gold ring to symbolize the blessedness is exquisite, beyond all joy and better than any possessions, just as gold is the most valuable and precious metal.

Luther's Seal has become a widely recognized symbol for Lutheranism and depicts the theology of Martin Luther and the Reformation.

Diet of Worms

I had no intention of writing to this extent about Luther, but once I got into it, one point led to another, and I feel I should conclude with a summary of the Diet of Worms, which was called by Charles V and to which Luther was summoned in response to a papal bull by Pope Leo X.

Prince Frederick III, elector of Saxony, obtained an agreement that if Luther appeared, he would be promised safe passage to and from the meeting. At the assembly, Luther's writings—twenty-five books—were challenged, and it was demanded that he renounce or reaffirm them. Luther responded that he would if shown by Scripture that he was in error. In conclusion, Luther refused and said, "Here I stand. I can do no other."

Luther was declared a "notorious heretic," and reading or possession of his books was banned.

Frederick III had no faith in the letter of safe conduct to and from the hearing given to Luther. Fearing for his life, Frederick sent men to fake a highway attack and abduct Luther, hiding him away at Wartburg Castle. Frederick's premonition was correct as the Diet issued an edict by Emperor Charles V declaring:

> For this reason we forbid anyone from this time forward to dare, either by words or deeds, to receive, defend, sustain, or favour the said Martin Luther. On the contrary, we want him to be apprehended and punished as a notorious heretic, as he deserves, to be brought personally before us, or to be securely guarded until those who have captured him inform us, whereupon we will order the appropriate manner of proceeding against the said Luther. Those who will help in his capture will be rewarded generously for their good work.

There is a striking statue of Luther in Worms.

CHAPTER 8

Honeymoon Discoveries

*R*eggie and Sapphire, newlyweds, were undressing in preparation for their first marital encounter and when Reggie removed his shoes and stockings Sapphire noticed his toes were quite
shriveled. "Reggie, honey, whatever happened to your toes?" "Oh,
I had toemain poisoning when I was young." When he dropped his
trousers, Sapphire noticed with dismay, "Reggie, what happened
to your knees?" "Oh," replied Reggie, I had kneemonia when I was
young." Moments later Sapphire gushed relief, "Oh, Reggie, thank
goodness, I was so afraid you might have had dicktheria, too!"

Summers on the farms

While I usually spent my boyhood summers at Uncle Richard's,
cousin Dick and I were just three months apart in age, I well remember one summer at Uncle Jack's in Bear Creek. That is near
Sugar Bush where I was picked up at the train station, having
taken the milk train from Neenah. Sugar Bush had a feed mill and
a pickle factory. You'll never find more contented cows than those
who are fed ground wheat and silage.

I always thought Uncle Jack was my dad's step brother because he was a Thomack, too, but my sister said they were cousins. I asked why we called him "Uncle Jack" and she said, "It's because he married Aunt Alma." Aunt Alma and our mother were sisters. Jack and Alma had two children, Wesley and Gladys, four years and two years older than I was.

I had my first driving experience there one day when Wes and I were out in the potato field knocking potato bugs off the plants. With a cedar shingle we'd catch the bugs in a five gallon pail. It was a very hot and humid day and Wes told me to take the car, a Model T Ford, to go fetch more cold coffee from the house. I told him I had never driven but he assured me I'd do just fine and away I went. There's a deep ditch running alongside the road with a culvert by the farm entrance and I was really going too fast to make the turn but careened over it and nearly struck one of the poplar trees lining the driveway. Aunt Alma happened to be looking out and saw me coming. Her jaw dropped and eyes grew wide open, probably wider than mine were. Somehow I managed to brake just short of the pig sty.

Aunt Alma canned meats, beef and venison, in two quart Mason jars. I didn't care much for the beef but it was better than the venison that was just awful tasting to me. There is a cedar swamp on the farm property and that is where Uncle Jack hunted the deer so may have affected the flavor. I don't know what spice she added but it may have been bay leaf which I still don't care for. Years later I was given some venison chops in Kentucky and how I loved them.

One day I stepped on a large rusty nail that poked all the way through my foot. Uncle Jack took some tobacco he was chewing, put it on my foot and packed cow manure on top of that to draw out any infection and to prevent blood poisoning. Did the trick!

There was a cheese factory about a mile from the farm and Uncle Jack hauled his milk there as all the local farmers did. The cans of milk were loaded onto a big wagon pulled by King and Queen, his team of horses. Behind the factory stood an ice house, a barn-like structure. Huge blocks of ice cut from frozen lakes were stored in the loft and packed in saw dust. It was amazing the ice never melted despite the summer heat.

Aunt Alma made ice cream and I have yet to find any that tastes better than hers did. At times she added freshly ripened strawberries for an added treat.

I've always loved animals of all kinds so it really bothered me when the pigs were slaughtered. The pigs were shot in the head and their throats slit. The blood was collected to make blood sausage (I never tried it). You can imagine what head cheese was made of.

Uncle Jack had a team of horses, King and Queen. One day Queen was going to be bred and when the stud service arrived I was sent to the farmhouse. I was deemed too young to witness the action. I detoured and hid in the grainery to watch the goings on. That was my introduction to animal husbandry and I would later witness similar activity by pigs, cows, ducks. etc. I was fortunate to be there when Queen delivered a beautiful colt, Prince, but it lived only three days.

The pharmacist was giving a woman instructions for use of a product she was purchasing. "Apply it to your arms twice a day" he said when the woman cut him off. "It's not for my arms. It's for my schnauzer" she bristled. "Oh, in that case," retorted the pharmacist, "apply it three times a day and don't take a bath for a week."

Kentucky Explosion

Thadeus and Bertha were driving through the hills of Kentucky when Bertha quite suddenly had need of rest room facilities. "Taddy", she cried, "you have to hurry because I really have to get to a bathroom right now!" "Bertha, you know I'm driving as fast as I can....if you can't hold it you'll just have to hang it out the window and let it fly." She had no choice and....SPLAAAAT!... she plastered two hillbillies standing along the roadside waiting for the car to pass.

Clem says to Fletch, "What in tarnation whar that?" "Danged if I know but you see the set of jaws on that critter?"

High School

Would I be correct if I said "education" is a segmented process? We have grade school, junior high, high school, college and … job training and experience, as I perceive it. I had little sense of escalation from grade school to high school, unlike the jump from high school to college. High school seemed relatively easy and seldom required true homework, as the assignments could readily be completed in study hall if I applied myself.

Ivan Williams taught American History and was the tennis coach. He also directed the city tennis tournaments sponsored by the recreation department. I thought he was a little whippy. In history classes, remembering the exact date of an event seemed as important as the event itself. While I handle numbers with ease, historical dates were different. Nevertheless, my grades in the classes were very good.

Ms. Lila Raines and J. D. Shepard were mathematics teachers. Mr. Shepard was a tall, handsome guy in his first year of teaching. He dressed more casually than other teachers; slacks and loafers defined his wardrobe. Of course, all the girls were gaga over him. He taught the higher math courses: algebra and trigonometry.

To me, geometry was the easiest "math" course. Ms. Raines was the only teacher who ever gave me an F on a homework assignment. I went to see her about that, and she said someone else had completed the work, because she hadn't yet taught us the solution employed. I explained that I knew it from grade school, and she gave me the grade I earned after I told her I went to Trinity.

Ms. Ruth Thompson and Edna Harris were English teachers. Ms. Thompson ridiculed and embarrassed me in front of the class for a book report I gave. The book was a Western novel by Zane Grey. "Zane Grey? Zane Grey?" she almost shouted. "Who is Zane Grey?"

"Well," I answered, "I really don't know, but I certainly enjoyed the book, and that's more important to me than the person who wrote it." I thought she was totally out of order and unprofessional.

Note: The first real book I recall reading was many years earlier, when I might have been eleven or twelve years old. The title was *Space Ship to Saturn*. To me, it was memorable because it described rocket launchings exactly as they happen, with the lift-off, pitch, and roll. I'm not an avid reader, but I found excitement in that book, and it did create an interest in finding enjoyable readings.

Edna "Ma" Harris was quite a large, heavy older woman. My boyhood friend, Tom, sat next to me, and I think this was the only class we had together. He leaned over by me and said, "She just picked up that dress at Oshkosh Tent & Awning." Years later, it was rumored OTA was Hilary's source for some of the horse blankets she was known to wear.

Mr. John Gundlach was the biology teacher, and what I most remember from his class is the smell of formaldehyde the poor little frog I dissected was pickled in. Gundlach's son was our best running back, and I was the lead blocker for him.

Emma Kiser (rhymes with *riser*) was also an older teacher, the stereotypical old maid, who might have been a relative of the prune family. She was very stoic—and perhaps appropriately so, as this was my foreign language study, Latin. I chose it because a foreign language was required as part of the college preparatory program I was pursuing, and I didn't want any part of German. Many English words are of Latin derivation.

Ms. Kiser was ill one day, so a substitute teacher came in. She asked, "How do you pronounce your teachers' name—*Miss Kisser?*" It was hard for us to get serious for the remainder of the day. As straightlaced as she was, Ms. Kiser did teach us to sing "Hail, Hail, the Gang's All Here" in Latin:

> Eo eo omnes ad sunc
> Quid curie es nobis
> Quid curie es nobis
> Eo Eo omnes ad sunc
> Quid curie es nobes nunc.

George Christoph was the manual arts instructor and also helped with intramural athletics. He was built like Man Mountain. I didn't take a manual arts class but later wished I had, for the practical knowledge one can apply in life situations. I think it should be a required course for all male students, just as home economics was required for female students. Eventually, I would rent one of Mr. Christoph's properties.

Mr. Floyd Cummings was our student guidance counselor— and in name only, as far as I was concerned, because I never got any counseling, even with my being in the college preparatory program. I wouldn't say he was effeminate, but he didn't strike me as being very macho. My one meeting with him had nothing to do with academics. I was summoned to his office, because he observed me dancing too close with my date and felt that could lead to trouble.

Just as the freight train was coming out of the tunnel, Casper, the engineer, saw a couple lying in the middle of the tracks ahead and blew the train whistle to warn them of the approaching train. The couple didn't move.

Casper blew the whistle three more times before hitting the emergency brakes and screeching to a stop only a few feet from the couple, Rastus and Zinnia, who were still entwined.

Casper, who was hopping mad, jumped down and shouted, "You damn fools. You could have been killed. Why didn't you get out of the way?"

"Man," said Rastus, "You was coming, and I was coming, and you was the only one with brakes."

Back to Camp

After Boys' Brigade camp, Onaway Island operated the remainder of the summer with a maintenance man, a cook, and six chore boys who were usually chosen from the top high school athletes.

For some unknown reason, the current group was summarily dismissed shortly after the start of the season, and I was among the group recruited to replace them.

Becoming a chore boy was a distinguishing honor sought after and a great opportunity, as you spent the summer with close friends working as a unit and sharing experiences that bonded you to each other. Red, Whitey, Neil, Jack, Kip, and I would spend two summers together under the rule of Ma Dick, the camp cook. Our quarters were an adjunct to the main pavilion during the first summer, but we occupied a new cottage the following year. The maintenance man lived alone in a similar cabin. He was also the latrine orderly.

New camping groups, usually from Lutheran churches from in and out of state, arrived on Sunday afternoons and broke camp the following Saturdays. Chore boys helped them move in and get situated in their tents. Our regular duties were devoted primarily to meal preparation, serving, and bussing the tables.

The hymn-singing before and after the evening meals was truly wonderful and reminded me of the glorious music from the upper-class kids that echoed through the halls at Trinity. Ma Dick had been the cook for years, so she was very experienced in cooking for large groups, here 100 to 150, according to her menus developed over that time and favored by the campers. Dessert was often cottage pudding, as she called it, and was usually smothered in one of her sweet, tasty sauces. Ma always cooked for our high school team athletic banquets, and the entrée was always the same: chicken à la king.

When our services weren't required in the kitchen, we were free to engage in whatever activity we wanted, but most of that time was spent on the basketball court or pitching horseshoes. Red was the best there. Red, Neil, and I made the high school varsity basketball team largely due to all the practice.

Saturdays were special and anticipated, because the campers

were gone by midafternoon at the latest, and we were free to follow our heart's desires. Ma usually prepared big T-bone steaks on the surface of the great wood-fired kitchen stove that had three ovens. After dinner, we took canoes to Edmund's Boat Dock a good distance away, beached them, and hitchhiked into Waupaca for a movie. Then we would hitchhike back, race each other back to the island, strip naked, and plunge into the lake around midnight.

One night, I swam out a distance, rolled onto my back, and glanced over my shoulder, only to see a snake wriggling toward me in the reflection of the moonlight on the glass-smooth water. Johnny Weismueller would have been a distant second to me reaching the dock. Last time for nighttime swims!

Joretta Chermak and Jodell Schmidt … Wow! Joretta was so, so beautiful, dark with long, luxuriant hair. Jodell was blonde, athletic, also quite pretty, and an outstanding tennis player. Red saw Joretta first and latched onto her. Her church group was from Manitowoc, only twenty miles distant from Sheboygan, and I often thought of contacting her for old time's sake. That would not have been very difficult, because her family owned Chermak Sausage Company, well-known for a variety of quality meat products.

Remember the girl with Shirley Temple curls I had a crush on in the second grade? She and several of her friends came to visit us in August—the same week of Japan's unconditional surrender. How fortunate I was to have such an opportunity so few were privileged to experience. Thanks, Boys' Brigade!

Playing the Game

Everybody who plays a sport will have days when they find themselves in a zone, whether it is basketball, tennis, golf, tiddlywinks, or whatever. I could throw in competitive and exhibition diving as well, because I had days when I hit the board pretty well. You keep playing these games over in your mind.

Note: The US Olympic swimming and diving team trained in Neenah before the Olympics, and I believe it was in 1948. Dr. Sammy Lee was the champion diver, and I was able to watch some of his workouts. His coach would call out the dive to perform after he started his approach—I imagine so he didn't change his takeoff for a particular dive.

He competed in the three-meter springboard and ten-meter platform diving events, winning back-to-back gold medals in platform diving. He was of Korean descent and became an eye, ear, nose, and throat doctor. Dr. Lee died in 2016 at age ninety-six.

Neenah was considered a basketball school, and its longtime coach, Ole Jorgensen, was considered one of the best coaches in the state, as he took teams to state rather regularly. I was an underclassman when Neenah made it to the championship game with a dream team that had size and talent. Madison West was the opponent, and Neenah played a lousy first half, really came back in the second half, but fell just short.

Darrel Schultz was the team captain and probably the best Rocket to wear the red and white uniform. He played at LSU under scholarship. I guess Coach didn't see that in our future, as I thought he was quite passive in coaching us, and we weren't prepared for the opponent's strengths or how to play against them. More on that point later. He did say, "I'll never criticize you for shooting too much, just at the wrong time." He didn't explain what the "wrong time" would be.

When it was time to report for basketball my freshman year, Coach Jorgensen asked whether Neil Christopherson and Frank Wegman were present. They were outstanding players on St. Patrick's, and I suppose he thought they might wind up at Menasha St. Mary's. Red and I were unknown to him, but all four of us made the freshman squad. Wegman didn't get much playing time and was off the team in our senior year. I was the only starter as a junior, and I teamed with Clint to make what was called the outstanding guard tandem in the state. He went on to have a standout career at Ripon College.

During our first practice session as freshmen, Coach Jorgensen stressed one thing: You never throw a cross-court pass in front of your opponent's basket. His star player committed that error; the pass was intercepted, and the resulting score cost the team the state championship.

Still in my freshman year, we played our final game of the season at Menasha, our archrival. Menasha had a new facility that was as fine as any in the state. There was a swimming pool beneath the court, and we took advantage of it after the game. As we were leaving, we found a basketball game in progress, and we laughed at the big bunch of hay-shakers who didn't know what a bounce pass or a chest pass was, as they made two-handed overhead passes, so all the passes were over the top. The game was a qualifier for regional tournament play. The team, Reedsville, went on to win the state title and at least three of the players—Behnke, Kuballe, and Barnard—went on to college ball.

Senior year, we were playing at Shawano, which always floored a good basketball team, and I had a memorable game for two reasons: the first was that I was in a zone and every shot was falling for me, and the second was about a steal I made. Red was slow getting back on defense and already well ahead of me when I threw him a lead pass. He was loping up the court and gradually turned his head to look back over his shoulder. At that instant, the ball was coming straight at his head. He ducked, and the ball flew out of bounds.

I lost it. I just cracked up and could hardly stay on my feet as we played on. I don't think Red ever forgave me for that.

Just as you have memorable games, you have games you'd rather forget. This particular game was at Kaukauna, after we beat them at home. During the home game, I can't explain why, I put a form tackle on Cliff Hinkens, the Kaukauna star, as he was driving in for a layup and put him flat on his back at the free throw line. The Galloping Ghosts were waiting for me when we played there. They double-teamed me and were grabbing my legs. As I tried to get my legs free, I was called for kicking. After a brief conference with the Kaukauna bench, I was ejected from the game.

It seems basketball rules are constantly changing, and personally, I think the current rule allowing players to take a charge is totally wrong and leads to more judgment calls when we already have too many pauses in a game as officials take time for reviews. We were taught the player with the ball has a right to a path to the basket, and he is defenseless as he leaves his feet. A player can still defend but not deliberately take a charge. I marvel that there aren't more serious injuries. I doubt I'd want to be playing today, as this is not the way the game should be played. What do you say, Naismith?

It was my senior year, and our regional tournament game was coming up in two days. As I was walking down the hallway, Coach Jorgensen spotted me coming with my head cranked to the side. During the previous night, I had turned over in bed and something twisted in my back. I thought it might be a latent football injury.

Coach took me to a chiropractor for an adjustment and got me straightened out. Our opponent was Kimberly, which always had exceptionally tall players. Red, our center, was only a hair over six feet tall. We knew nothing about Kimberly except that for years, it had been running up unheard-of scores for high school basketball. Real run-and-gunners.

The first man to get the ball in the front court put it up. We played a slower, control-style game. Well, Kimberly's starting lineup included a six-foot-ten-inch center, Vanden Boom, and a jumping jack, Rusty Tiedeman, who had a jump shot, which hadn't yet become popular. He just poured them in, and when they needed points, they just lofted the ball into the center for easy scores. We suffered our worst defeat of the season. Tiedeman went onto have a tremendous college career in baseball and basketball at Oshkosh University.

It's customary during the team's breakup session for the outgoing players to elect a captain for the following season. As I was the only returning starter, it was a foregone conclusion that it would be me—so it was something of a surprise when Red and I were named co-captains. I was already co-captain of the football team for the next season, and I didn't expect that, although I did receive a scholarship offer from a small college in Michigan. Dating Cliff's ex-girlfriend, our head cheerleader, didn't win me the "most popular fellow" award, and I understood that.

Back in my playing days, you played both sides of the ball. I was the fullback on offense and a linebacker on defense. It was traditional to play our archrival, Menasha, in the season finale, and that's when you want to have your best game. Menasha actually helped me do that. There were such big gaps between the offensive linemen that I virtually lined up in them myself and was able to make tackle after tackle in the backfield as the running back was taking the handoff.

I think I invented the "red dog" that night. I caught a pass over the middle for a score, but my usual roll on offense was as a lead blocker. We were taught cross-body blocking, and that was really tough on my ribs. After the game, the Menasha speedster tailback told me he was surprised I was as fast as I was, as I covered him on pass plays and he couldn't shake me. One of my sisters would marry his brother. I ruined a good game by missing two extra points, but we had plenty to win without them.

Everything changes, doesn't it? Even in sports, after years and years of competition. Recently, I was watching a college football game when a big lineman's pants somehow got pulled down and his butt was exposed. His crack split the TV screen briefly before a teammate pulled them back up. The pants must have had an elastic band to hold them in place. We wore a belt, so that never happened, but we also wore hip pads, thigh pads, kneepads, and high shoes. Our shoulder pads were so big you had to turn sideways to exit the dressing room. We had soft leather helmets with no chin strap or face guard, and we didn't have mouthpieces.

Gloves? I can't imagine wearing gloves. If you have soft hands, you don't need them, and I think receivers would do better without them.

Commencement Exercises

Scholarships were awarded at graduation, but I was not a recipient of any, even though I ranked third in the class behind two girls: Kathryn Schultz, who was the dentist's daughter, and Nancy Neller. I was a National Honor Society member but was never questioned about my interest in college, despite my having been enrolled in the college preparatory program. Well done, student counselor Floyd Cummings!

Stock tip: Victoria's Secret and Smith & Wesson are merging. The new company is going to be called Titty Titty Bang Bang.

My next foray into organized basketball was at the University of Wisconsin Fieldhouse as I walked on for tryouts, which I don't think is possible anymore without an invitation to do so. I was having a good game and outplaying the current Wisconsin Mr. Basketball. After a break, I was inserted back into the game, grabbed the tip, and drove in for a layup. Somehow, I missed it when they changed goals, and I put the ball in the wrong basket. Dang! I knew that was the end for me, and I never returned. Even if they had any interest in me, the coaches had no idea who I was.

I got back into basketball after getting out of college and the military. Gord's Tavern and Ollie's Tavern were teams in the Industrial League, which featured quite a few outstanding players. Red played for Ollie's, and I was on Gord's roster, so Red and I were no longer teammates but rivals. I never considered him to be a team player, as it was all about himself.

Box scores were published in the local newspaper, and Coach Jorgensen must have become curious about our new scoring prowess, as I spotted him at one of our games against Ollie's. The only practice we had was the pregame warm-ups, yet we were playing well. I was named MVP several times in tournaments we won. Gord's team was coached by Ken LaBombard and assisted by Ralph Parker, my father-in-law's stepbrother and brother, respectively.

Red eventually joined the air force, attended the University of Mexico City thereafter, and married the daughter of a wealthy businessman out east. He never attended a class reunion and died in his early sixties.

Back to the game of basketball: A defender came hard at me as I was driving down the lane, and as he knocked me off my feet, I grabbed him around the neck to break my fall. I thought I had my arm around a tree trunk. Yes, he was a big, burly fellow.

Later in the game, there was a loose ball I went after. The same player who hit me earlier threw a roll block into me and pinned my shoulder to the floor, breaking my collarbone. There's no way to immobilize a broken clavicle, so the slightest movement or even just a deep breath causes terrible pain. My wife and I slept head to foot for three weeks to avoid the possibility of her rolling over on me.

I never broke another bone, but there were other things I hoped to never experience: open-heart surgery, brain surgery, ice baths, eye surgery, and strokes. How did I miss shingles and the gout in that list? I haven't had a good batting average.

Deke and Zeke decided to visit a house of ill repute. The madam couldn't get any of her girls to accommodate the boys because they were so repulsive, with greasy long hair, shaggy beards, wild eyes, and few teeth.

Not wanting to lose the business, the madam remembered there were two inflatable dolls in the attic and told Deke and Zeke how to find the "girls."

Afterward, Deke asked Zeke how it was for him and Zeke said, "It was like nothing. She was cold, just laid there and never moved."

Deke said, "Mine was the very same, except I think I had a witch. When nothing was happening, I nipped her on her breast to get a rise out of her, and she flew out the window."

Then there was a whore who couldn't spell. She spent two weeks in a warehouse.

A Greenwich Village theater had a somewhat cult patronage, as it usually featured bohemian-style movies. The coming week's attraction was a trio of Shakespearean plays. Rupert, the theater manager, gave the play list to Joe, the maintenance man, to put on the marquee.

Upon returning from an errand, Rupert was shocked to see *Three Inches*, *Six Inches*, and *Nine Inches* displayed instead of the movie titles.

"What on earth is this all about?" he demanded of Joe.

Joe explained that there wasn't enough room to show the titles, but he'd come up with a solution to the problem.

"What is *Three Inches* supposed to be?" queried Rupert.

"Why, that's *Much Ado About Nothing*."

"How about *Six Inches*?"

"Why, that's *As You Like It*."

Distraught and hesitant to inquire further, Rupert did pose the question, "What's *Nine Inches*?"

Joe smiled and chided, "Rupert, I thought you knew your Shakespeare. *Nine Inches*, of course, is for *Taming of the Shrew*." And Rupert fainted.

It was Hell Week, and hazing had been banned after some tragic occurrences. Malcomb was eager to be a part of fraternity life, as his father had told him of the wonderful lifetime friends he made as a member. Malcomb knew all about hazing but was willing to endure just about anything to gain acceptance. He would show them he had the right stuff and would be an asset to the organization. He thought it would be a breeze for him when he could prove his worth by spending a night in a field, naked and tied to a tree.

When they came to retrieve Malcomb the following morning, they found him limp and almost lifeless. "You OK, Malcomb? What happened to you?"

Barely able to speak, Malcomb asked, "Doesn't that calf have a *mother*?"

It was either at the Chamber of Commerce banquet or at a Kiwanis Club windup that a Jewish comedian was to be the featured entertainment. He sat looking like an old toad until the introduction, when he immediately morphed into his stage persona. I remember two of his offerings:

Felix and Bernard were close friends since childhood days and remained such all through college, like when they both earned doctor degrees, Felix as a psychiatrist and Bernard as a proctologist. They decided to share office space initially, as that would cut overhead expenses in half.

Thinking a theme or motto would help attract business, they considered "Odds and Ends," "Nuts and Butts," and "Rears and Queers." In time, they went their separate ways, as their growing practices required more spacious accommodations.

Some time thereafter, Felix spotted Bernard approaching as he was out running an errand. "Hey, Bernard," called Felix, "how's it going?"

Bernard put his thumb and index finger together to form an *o*, put it up to his eye, and said, "Looking up!"

The rabbi was ready to perform the circumcision when he discovered the scissors was missing from his satchel and asked the woman of the house for a pair. She had only a pinking shears, and that's how Aaron wound up with the frilliest dilly in town.

Recently, I had to have a COVID-19 test, as I was scheduled for cataract surgery in a few days. After administering the test, the nurse said, "I never dreamed I'd be looking up so many nostrils."

My quick response was, "Well, you could have been a proctologist."

Pastor Martin reserved two days each week to call on the elderly, shut-ins, and hospitalized. Today he visited Mrs. Murphy and announced, "I'm here to talk about the hereafter."

"Oh, thank goodness, Pastor Martin. Every time I walk into another room, I ask myself, *What am I here after?*"

Three elderly sisters lived together. Elsie said she was worried about her sisters. Eunice was up in the bathroom and didn't know if she was getting in or out of the bathtub. "Look, there's Louise on the stairs. She doesn't know if she's going up or down the steps. Thank goodness I've still got all my wits about me. Knock on wood." Knock, knock, knock. "Come in!"

Pool Time

I practically lived at the swimming pool the summer before my senior year of high school. I passed the life-saving program and became a lifeguard while still involved in competitive, exhibition, and synchronized diving. My partner in synchronized diving was my Greek buddy, Jimmy, and we matched well because we were built alike. We did our act from twin diving boards and did identical or opposite dives.

There were always plenty of girls hanging around, and Rosemary Schwebs from Menasha was just about a daily feature. She had beauty and was statuesque. She always wore a one-piece black swimming suit that had a neck strap she untied and twirled in her hand. Personally, I think a one-piece swimming suit does more for a woman's body than the two-piece bikini things.

She also had talent. Twirling came naturally to her, and her talent was taking her to Ohio State to strut her stuff before the Buckeye fans. She was usually the entertainment at halftime of the Menasha high school basketball games. She could twirl her batons from any position and even twirled twin batons simultaneously.

With the lights turned off, she tossed flaming batons high into the air and never had a miscue. Of course, she saw me during my diving exhibitions and told me I should consider going to Ohio State, too, but I didn't think my back and reverse dives were strong enough. They didn't come naturally to me.

Another girl who made daily appearances at the pool was the gal I sat next to in study hall. Janet always gave me notes to give to her boyfriend and my friend, Frank. I never saw Janet or Rosemary in the water. Before summer's end, Janet and I were going steady, and she would be my prom date with a gardenia corsage. In time, we would go our separate ways because of religious differences, but the parting wouldn't last forever.

CHAPTER 9

College Bound

With high school graduation on the immediate horizon, it was still my intention to get a college education, but I lacked the financing for it and planned to work for a year before matriculating. I was wondering how and where to look for employment when I was notified I'd been recommended for a job in a research lab that Marathon Corporation was looking to fill. I was one of three candidates, with the other two coming from Menasha St. Mary's and Appleton High School. Whether by selection or default, I got the job.

I became familiar with all the operators in the carton plant, the flexible packaging plant, and the wax plant. I needed a good rapport with them to persuade them to break into their production to run samples for me.

One morning, there was commotion back by the boss's office, and we heard screaming and banging noises. We all ran back there to investigate and found the boss's secretary all doubled up in laughter. Finally, she was able to explain what had happened. She thought a mouse was running up her leg, and that's when she screamed and kicked her wastebasket across the room. The "mouse" was merely a run in her nylons.

Old Mel Grant, a really nice man who was so helpful to me, had worked in the research department for years and was on the verge of retirement. He told me about the guy who had a hemorrhoidectomy, which required periodic visits with the surgeon to get reamed out to promote proper healing. After several visits, he asked the doctor if his wife couldn't do the reaming to save his having to make ongoing trips to the office, and the doctor consented.

The patient then explained the process to his wife. "You put your right hand on my right shoulder ... no, you put your left hand on my left shoulder ... why, that dirty son of a bitch!"

Payday came twice a month, and that was tough when you had three weekends on one pay period. I allowed myself five dollars out of each payday and banked the balance. Mr. Ward, my bank president, sent me a personal letter congratulating me for my savings record. Moneywise, I'd have been better off to have taken a factory job in the plant like my buddies did. They were making twice as much money as I was.

And, finally, off to college.

University of Wisconsin

It was in 1950 that I enrolled at the University of Wisconsin Madison. I was assigned to the Adams Hall dormitory and had a fellow by the name of Robert Goodsitt for a roommate. His family owned the Mamma and Pappas restaurant in Milwaukee. Meals were included in the dorm rent and were served in the freestanding cafeteria, which served other dormitory residents as well. The quality of the food was very good.

My oldest sister, Gert, managed the soda fountain at a

Rennebohm Drug Store. Rennebohm was a pharmacist before becoming governor of the state of Wisconsin. Gert got me a part-time job at the drugstore, and that would cause me to change the direction of my studies at a later date. For the present, I was enrolled in the pre-pharmacy program. It seemed most of the students had families already in the business. From what I learned in talking with some of the pharmacists, you didn't want to be a pharmacist unless you could own the pharmacy, because your workdays were 24-7. Furthermore, I didn't find organic chemistry very exciting.

The first semester was a struggle for me. High school had been so easy; I really didn't have to apply myself, and I didn't know how to take good class notes. Also, I didn't like reviewing past material, which was key to attaining good grades, because final exams were weighted so heavily against final grades, accounting for 50 to 70 percent depending on the course and the instructor.

Some students relied on finals to raise their grades, as they really crammed for them. However, exam schedules could create a problem, like having them all fall within two days. There was no option to change the schedule unless you had three exams in one day. Dorm life was not conducive to good study habits for me, and I moved into a private rooming house until I joined a fraternity, Tau Kappa Epsilon (TKE), and took a single room there. My lunch and dinner meals were provided by the sorority I worked at, Delta Delta Delta.

Of all the classes I had, three stand out in my mind for various reasons:

❖ **Conversational Spanish**—I couldn't differentiate any words in the initial class. It went *la, la lala, lala, lala*, and I thought of dropping the class as I heard others opted for when they were in trouble grade-wise. But I stayed with it and actually earned an A and had a role in a

Spanish play the department produced. A fellow student, Cameron, encouraged me to hang in there and convinced me not to drop the course. I was able to maintain a 4.0 that semester.

❖ **Business statistics**—This was a class everyone dreaded having to take, but I breezed through it until the final exam. The proctor gave the start signal, and suddenly I froze up. I couldn't think of anything, and I was panicking. It took a full hour before I started to function, and then I went like crazy to finish the exam, saving my grade.

❖ **Business mathematics**—I really had to apply myself in this course and managed an A all the way through. After an exam, you usually have a good sense of how well you did, and I didn't have any concern after this one. So when I received the final grade in the mail, I was shocked to see I was given a D. That had to be a mistake. I called the instructor, who didn't appreciate being questioned, and in the end said he didn't make any mistakes.

Pedro, the old parrot, had a vocabulary laced with "blue" adjectives, and he delighted in shocking patrons of the tavern, especially first-time customers. The business was suffering as a result of Pedro's driving off the more genteel, and Sam was going to put an end to it.

He told Pedro, "You've driven away my best customers. I've warned you over and over, and this is the last time. You do that again, and I'm going to wring your neck."

Pedro, ever obstinate and incorrigible, thought he'd heard plenty of idle threats before, and this was just another one. Plus, after all, he'd been a fixture in the establishment long before Sam became the owner and couldn't wait to "welcome" the next new customer, as was his habit.

But Pedro misjudged Sam's resolve. After a well-dressed couple left abruptly when Pedro assailed them, Sam said, "Damn it, you miserable feathered buzzard. That's it!" He wrung Pedro's neck and threw him into the trash can out back.

A well over-served woman came reeling down the alley in desperate need of a comfort station. Finally, she spotted the trash can and perched upon it. The warm shower revived Pedro. He opened one eye, looked up, and declared, "Dang! If she can live with a gash like that, I can live with a broken neck."

Wisconsin Football

For the second semester of my senior year, I carried a reduced credit load so I could return for one more football season, leaving me to pick up a three-credit elective, as I had met the other requirements to earn a bachelor of business administration degree. I was going to have a fun fall. Isn't it strange how things can or don't happen? Marriage and military service changed my plans.

When it came to college football, Wisconsin was not a formidable opponent except for the Wisconsin–Minnesota game, which is the longest continuous rivalry in the NCAA. At one point, Minnesota led the series by twenty games, but the Badgers have come back to take the lead 62–60–8, having won fourteen in a row, until Minnesota pulled an upset at Madison in 2019.

Wisconsin last won a title in 1912, and in an effort to shore up the program, hired Harry Stuhldreyer, one of the Four Horsemen at Notre Dame, in 1937. In twelve years, Stuhldreyer went 45–62, just 2–7 in his final year, and he was fired.

Out of little-known Lafayette, Wisconsin, came Ivy Williamson, and in just six years he compiled a 41–19–4 record, winning Wisconsin's first title in 1952 after a forty-year drought. He lost the 1953 Rose Bowl to USC by a 7–0 score. Wisconsin had opportunities but couldn't capitalize on them, and USC held Alan Ameche, the Heisman trophy winner, to half of his seasonal average per carry.

Wisconsin was an outstanding defensive team, and it became known as the Hard Rocks. J. C. Caroline was tearing up the league, and the Badgers shut him down completely when the Illini came to Madison.

Williamson became the athletic director after the 1955 season, and his assistant, Milt Bruhn, was named successor. Bruhn's record was 52–45–6 in ten years, but he did win titles in 1959 and 1962. The NFL selected twelve Badgers in the 1960 draft.

Johnny Coatta, the quarterback of Williamson's 1952 Hard Rocks team, succeeded Bruhn but went just 3–26–1 in his two years, and Wisconsin football was back on its heels. John Jardine wasn't the answer, as he had a losing record, 37–47–3.

Now Dave McClain, an Ohio native and assistant coach under Bo Schembechler and Woody Hayes, was making great strides in turning Wisconsin in the right direction. His overall record was 46–42 in seven years, and he had the program heading north. He was the first Wisconsin coach to beat Michigan and Ohio State in the same season and was 4–4 against Ohio State. Unfortunately, McClain died of a heart attack in a sauna after his regular workout. It was 1985, and he was just forty-eight years old.

I guess you'd call Jim Hilles an interim coach, as his 3–9 record ended his career, and everything McClain had going on went for naught when Don Morton was hired in 1987 and brought his veer offense with him. He had a gaudy 6–27 three-year run.

Prospects weren't looking up when Barry Alvarez, who was hand-picked by Donna Shalala, Wisconsin chancellor, and All American Pat Richter, athletic director, went 1–10 in his first year but won the title in his third year and beat UCLA in the Rose Bowl. With his overall record of 118–73–4 from 1990 to 2005, Alvarez won three titles with his power football approach and was 8–3 in bowl games he led the teams to. Plus, he was 1–1 in bowl games he coached after abrupt departures by coaches Bret Bielema and Gary Anderson.

Alvarez was 5–7–1 versus Ohio State after winning four of the last six contests. Alvarez also came up with the motion W, which has become one of the most recognizable team logos after Wisconsin displayed some horrendous ones over the years.

Bret Bielema was Alvarez's assistant and was groomed to be his successor. Coaching from 2006–2012, Bielema sported a 68–24 record, maintained the power football game, won three titles, and was 2–4 in bowl games. He departed abruptly before the 2013 Rose Bowl game when Arkansas bypassed protocol and hired Bielema directly without permission to contact him. Bielema jumped at the chance, because he thought there was greater opportunity for him to achieve in the SEC. After fashioning a less-than-stellar 29–34 record, he was fired. After a nine-year hiatus from the Big 10, Bielema is returning as the head coach at Illinois.

Gary Anderson went 19–7 through 2013 and 2014 but left

before the Rose Bowl, just as Bielema had, leaving Alvarez, now athletic director, to return to the sidelines for the game.

Currently, Paul Chryst, a Madison, Wisconsin, native and former Badger quarterback, heads the program. He's 52–16 after just six seasons, and is 4–1 in bowl games by defeating Wake Forest 42–28 after quickly falling behind 14–0 in the Mayo Bowl, December 20, 2020. We expect Coach Chryst to have continued success.

The Rose Bowl

Wisconsin won the Big Ten title in 1952 under Ivy Williamson and was headed to the Rose Bowl—and so were we, five of us initially, three guys and two gals. I had no idea who the girls were, nor did I have any idea of how well my fraternity brothers, Art and Dave, knew them or even how the arrangement was made.

My brother, Wil, recently discharged from the army after serving as a tank commander in the Korean conflict, bought a new Oldsmobile after one of our younger sisters wrecked his Nash convertible in a mishap while he was giving her a driving lesson. She did well until she turned into our driveway and proceeded to pile into our dad's vehicle, which happened to be parked in her way, in one of those moments of panic inexperienced drivers are often subject to. Wil readily agreed to let me drive his car to California. I'm not sure I'd have done the same for him, but the proposition didn't come up, and I took his offer as a show of brotherly love. The plan was for me to leave Neenah early Christmas morning, pick up this Laura in Appleton, which was nearby, and head to Madison a hundred miles due south, where Art, Dave, and Bonita were waiting.

I got a call from Laura late Christmas Eve, and she was sobbing heavily. At the last minute, her parents decided it wasn't a good idea to entrust their daughter into the care of three guys for nearly two weeks. I called Dave to tell him so he could warn Bonita that she'd be alone with us and give her a chance to back out as well. Bonita was devastated but determined to go nevertheless, because she wanted to see her former roommate who had transferred to Southern Cal.

So I headed to Madison alone to pick up my riders. I was introduced to Bonita, and we hit the road. I drove down through Illinois and into Missouri before turning the wheel over to Dave. I don't remember Art doing any of the driving. I thought Dave was driving too fast through the hills and around sharp curves in the Ozarks, as it was nighttime and raining, so the visibility wasn't the best. He told me to relax, as he'd know of any oncoming traffic because the lights would reflect off the telephone wires overhead.

Safely out of the Ozarks, we charged across Oklahoma, with Amarillo, Texas, as our destination—1,000 miles from home and another 1,500 to go. We got situated in our motel rooms, grabbed some Tex Mex grub, and went to a Texas roadhouse to check out the cowgirls on the dance floor.

Back on the road again, it would take us another three days to reach California, and then only as far as Palm Springs. We were driving along in New Mexico with me behind the wheel when the Olds began to lose power. I shifted into a lower gear with no result. I was ready to blame Dave for pounding the car when he drove. If you can get sick from worrying, I about did at that point, worried about what was I going to tell my brother. Then suddenly, we came to a crest in the road, from which we could see a city far below. Talk about relief … The climb had been so gradual and the countryside so broad with no landmarks that we just hadn't realized we were even climbing. That city was White Sands, about 5,000 feet below.

We made just one remarkable stop before Palm Springs, and that was at the awesome, awesome Grand Canyon. Well, there was another thing that I remember. It wasn't really a stop, but as we drove through Flagstaff, it was odd to see Christmas decorations around without a snowy background. They just seemed out of place there.

It was quite late at night when we pulled into Palm Springs, where we stayed overnight before our last leg to Los Angeles, still about a hundred miles away. Palm Springs wasn't yet very populated, it seemed, but it was a wonderful sight in the moonlight, and I've always wished I could have bought some property there. Before us lay this great valley surrounded by high mountains, and it was the most peaceful setting, with the full moon illuminating the mountains like a halo around the low-lying plain.

There was a fine motel with a huge, inviting swimming pool. The next day, we settled in at the TKE house after meeting our brotherly hosts before we took off to do some shopping and sightseeing. We found that pedestrians had the complete right of way, as cars stopped well back every time we stepped into the street. I bought a pair of shoes at a men's store near Figueroa and Vine. The shoes had inch-thick soles, and I thought it was the California style.

Now, Dave was determined to go to Tijuana and begged to take the car himself, as no one else was interested. He was almost insistent, as he was sharing expenses. But I was equally insistent that wasn't going to happen, out of concern for my brother's car.

Later in the day—just the guys, as Bonita wasn't with us—we wandered into a cocktail lounge to have a few beers. After the second drink, I asked the barmaid if she'd care to have one with us. She poured a little glass full from a bottle of pink stuff under the bar. She explained it was her house cocktail. I put another twenty dollar bill on the bar, and she kept the whole thing.

Wisconsin was headquartered at the Hotel Roosevelt, and that's where we headed on New Year's Eve. We didn't expect it to be such a swanky, luxurious place, nor did we know at the time that it was built by Louis B. Mayer, Mary Pickford, Douglas

Fairbanks, and Sid Grauman, or that every actor of any renown wanted to be seen there.

None of us spent any money that night, as there were hospitality rooms sponsored by some generous alumni we didn't know, but they welcomed us. I didn't see any drinks other than martinis, and they were being stirred up in water pitchers. I don't recall anything of the evening other than having the first drink, but there must have been more, as I was still dressed the next morning when someone woke me. My new shoes were sitting on the floor next to the bed, and the toes were all scuffed up. My friends had hauled me back to the car, dragging me face-down. Somehow, they found the car key I had tucked away in the watch fob pocket of my trousers for safekeeping.

Now it was on to Pasadena, where we found our assigned seats for the Tournament of Roses Parade. We were anxiously awaiting the main event of the day but got engrossed in the parade with its majestic floats, magnificent horses, and beauty queens. The Wisconsin float featured Alice in Dairyland and was a good representation, considering the relatively short time for design and construction, whereas most floats had been on the drawing board and planned for the better part of a year.

I don't consider myself to be an excitable person, but have to admit my heart was pounding with the opening kickoff about to happen. It was No. 5 USC vs. No. 11 Wisconsin. The only score of the game was a twenty-two-yard pass in the third quarter to Al Carmichael from USC's backup quarterback, who came off the bench after starter Jim Sears sustained a knee injury.

This was the fewest points ever scored in a Rose Bowl game, but the rematch in 1963 would produce the most ever scored. Wisconsin outgained USC 353–233, with sophomore Alan "The Horse" Ameche running for 133 yards on twenty-eight carries as Wisconsin outrushed USC 211–48. Wisconsin got inside USC's twenty-five yard line five times but failed to score. USC got a key stop when UW quarterback Jim Haluska overthrew a pass to Harlan Carl at the end zone at the end of the game. Carl, who had tremendous speed, played only three minutes in the game because of a knee injury. Final score: USC 7 Wisconsin 0.

Haluska became a high school coach after a brief career in the NFL. He fashioned a nifty lifetime record of 206–60–4, winning twelve conference titles and three state titles.

Adam went into a candy store to buy chocolates to go along with the flowers he was giving his wife for her birthday. "How much for the turtles?" he inquired and responded, "Oh, my!" to the answer. Then he asked how much for the peanut clusters and had the same reaction: "Oh, my!" He asked, "How about the strawberry creams?" and learned they were just as expensive. Finally, he looked at the salesman and asked, "What's that big lump on your neck?"

"Well," replied the salesman, "it's a fatty tumor. Why do you ask?"

"Oh," said Adam, "I thought it might be your nuts. Everything else is so high here."

I'm going to jump ahead to the 1963 Rose Bowl game, considered one of college football's most memorable. Again, it was USC, ranked No. 1, vs. Wisconsin, ranked No. 2, with the national championship on the line. Wisconsin was favored by two points but was out of it early, down 42-14.

The kickoff was delayed fifteen minutes. USC didn't come out onto the field, while Wisconsin stood around, not knowing of the delay. USC had been made aware of it. It was the fourth quarter before Wisconsin got into rhythm and scored twenty-three points, only to lose 42-37. Ron Vander Kelen, UW quarterback and Big 10 Player of the Year, completed seventeen of twenty-one passes in that stretch, hitting All American Pat Richter eleven times for 163 yards and Lou Holland nine times for a game total 401 passing yards. Wisconsin had thirty-two first downs and had an apparent touchdown pass to Holland called back for a clipping penalty, which the Badgers vehemently protested.

Near the end of the game, Wisconsin was at USC's four-yard line when Vander Kelen tried to hit backup tight end Elmars Ezerins in the end zone. Ezerins ran the wrong route, and the pass was intercepted. Wisconsin forced USC to punt, and a bad snap resulted in a safety for Wisconsin, making it 42–30 at that point. Wisconsin drove forty-three yards after the free kick before Vander Kelen found Richter for a nineteen-yard score with one minute and nineteen seconds left in the game.

USC recovered the onside kick, lost twelve yards in three plays, and was forced to punt. It looked like Wisconsin had the kick blocked, but somehow the kicker got the ball around the defender's hip, and that was the final play of the game. Vander Kelen was named co-MVP with USC's Pete Beathard.

Back then, the football season opened with the College All Star Game at Soldiers Field in Chicago. The opponent was always the reigning NFL champion. Ron Vander Kelen led the All Stars to a 20–17 victory over the Green Bay Packers in August 1963 on a seventy-four-yard pass to Pat Richter. Vander Kelen was named MVP for this game as well. Richter eventually became the Wisconsin athletic director after being persuaded to leave an executive position with Oscar Mayer.

Homeward Bound

We left early in the morning on January 2, despondent after the devastating 7–0 loss to Southern Cal. Dave was insistent we stop in Las Vegas, which none of rest of us cared about doing, but we agreed to it in the end. For me, it was kind of a peace offering after refusing to allow him to take the car for a jaunt into Tijuana. We hung around while Dave went in to make a killing at the blackjack table, and it wasn't long before he appeared with look of despair about him, indicating he hadn't fared too well.

The fact was further confirmed when Dave became adamant about driving home nonstop from there. I had no intention of complying, and my resolve was solidified later that day when we came across a horrendous accident shortly after it had happened. Two vehicles had crashed head-on in the middle of the road at the top of a rise. There couldn't have been any survivors. The victims had been removed, but a woman's leg was still lying there, and the nylons she was wearing had just exploded. There were kids' toys and stuffed animals strewn all over the roadside.

When we stopped to eat something before checking into the hotel, Dave said he wasn't hungry. For that matter, none of us had much of an appetite, with the accident still so fresh on our minds. When we reached the hotel, Dave stubbornly refused to join us, saying he would sleep in the car. What could we do? It was obvious Dave had lost his ass at the blackjack table and was broke but wouldn't admit it or accept any money.

The scenario repeated itself over and over during the remainder of the trip, and he spent another night in the car. I have no idea how he kept warm, as I wasn't going to let him run the engine for warmth. All this created an unpleasant atmosphere, with Dave in a sullen mood, rarely speaking. However, we did manage, no bitterness ever resulted, and we maintained a very good friendship over the years to come, although we never spoke of the Las Vegas incident again.

Why does it seem to take longer to get to an outbound destination than the return trip? Is it anticipation?

I learned from Dave that Art eventually became dean of a small college in Kentucky. Dave went on to law school after military service and became a very successful lawyer, setting precedents for some cases he won. Dave's father deserted his mother, head nurse at a Racine Hospital, when he was just an infant. Turns out his father was a full-blooded Native American, and Dave managed to locate him in Seattle while he was stationed in the area. Dave became dedicated to the plight of Indians and actually became president of a prominent national Indian organization.

Dave was a very good-looking dude and always made an effort to establish a good rapport with the jurors sitting on his cases, which probably didn't hurt his chances for winning some of them. I'm just surmising that and certainly hope I'm wrong, because Dave was capable of winning cases without such persuasion.

Once his practice was firmly established, Dave hosted an annual luau on his home premises, inviting six hundred clients and some friends, including me. His spacious grounds were terraced, with a small river running along the lower boundary. There were always four or five beer points going, corn being roasted over a bed of coals, and several pigs turning on spits manned by "volunteers." The corn was donated, as were the pigs and the manpower to run the show, as payment in kind from clients who couldn't pay the legal fees they owed. Most of the crew consisted of clients performing services in lieu of cash payments.

Dave's success came as something of a surprise to me and some others, I'm sure. It would be unkind to suggest it wasn't expected, and I don't mean that as it might sound. I'm pleased for him and pleased to have him for a friend. I always maintain one can have a lot of acquaintances, but true friends are to be treasured.

Back on Campus

School resumed, and I didn't date much, as I was still carrying a torch for my high school sweetheart after we broke up over religious differences. There was a girl who attracted me, but I think mostly because she reminded me of Janet. Jane K. was the gal from Wauwatosa, and I did get a date with her. She was living at Elizabeth Waters, a girls' dormitory. When I called her on the telephone, her roommate answered and said Jane would be with me in a minute, as she was doing the wash. When Jane came to the phone, I said, "Gee, I never heard of a washing machine that flushed." I guess you'd call that getting off on the wrong foot.

I asked a former girlfriend, Audrey, to my fraternity's annual "Shipwrecked" party. She was attending the University of Wisconsin La Crosse and majoring in physical education and modern dance. She spent the weekend with me in Madison, but the sparks weren't there anymore, at least for me. I don't know how she felt, but she still makes occasional contact with me to this day. We did have a fun weekend, and it was good to spend some time together again.

Now I was in my senior year, carrying a reduced credit load for what should have been my last semester on campus. But I wanted to return for one more football season. Wisconsin would fashion a 7–2 record in 1954.

Home for the summer in Neenah, I went downtown on a Friday night, which is when it seems just about everybody in town can be seen, and who do I meet but Janet? She was meeting some friends at a nearby cocktail lounge and asked if I'd like to join them. Of course I would, because I'd be with her again after a nearly four-year break.

Charlene was one of the gals in the group, and I could see the disapproval she displayed with looks at Janet. Charlene and Janet grew up together, and their parents were friends, too. They were close neighbors, and their houses were in view of each other.

Well, it turned out Janet was engaged to Frank, who had joined the air force, and Charlene and her guy, Jackson, often double-dated with Janet and Frank. He was the guy Janet always wrote notes to in high school study hall and gave them to me to pass on to Frank when I'd see him.

You can see what's coming here, and it didn't take long for that to happen. Janet broke her engagement to Frank and wore my fraternity pin on her bra until she finally informed her parents we were back together. Our wedding was set for November 27. My summer employment was as a pressman's helper in the flexible packaging manufacturing division of Marathon Corporation, and Janet was a private secretary to a Kimberly-Clark executive. I stayed on the job instead of returning to Madison.

Newspapers reported details of weddings back then, in which attendants, flowers in the bridal bouquet, a description of the bride's dress, and so on were noted. This is how Janet's attire was described in the *Oshkosh Daily Northwestern*: "The white gown worn by the bride was fashioned of rosepoint lace and nylon tulle over satin and was styled with a fitted bodice featuring long pointed sleeves and a V neckline. The bouffant skirt extended into a short lace train. A pearl-trimmed crown held the elbow length tulle veil in place. A white orchid and lilies-of-the-valley formed the bridal bouquet. The attendants were dressed identically in waltz-length frocks ..."

Next came the wedding reception, which was an expression of the bride's parents' "approval" of our wedding. It was held at the YWCA, where coffee, tea, and cookies were served by several of Janet's girlfriends. How can I describe how unhappy my male relatives were with that? In plain English, *pissed off.*

Then it was time for the cake-cutting which didn't amount to much either, as the cake was something like an oversized cupcake. And then we were away for our honeymoon, from which we returned to an apartment we had rented in Appleton. It was sufficient for a temporary living quarters until I had to report for military service.

CHAPTER 10

Military Service

S ummer camp was a requirement of the ROTC program and preceded Officer Candidate School (OCS). My recollection of summer camp is quite vague, possibly because it wasn't a pleasant experience, but several things linger in my mind. One was the marches in the heat and humidity. The other had to do with a white-glove inspection we seemed totally prepared for. A weekend pass hung in the balance, and we hadn't had one to this point.

Three players from the Wisconsin football team were in our unit: center Gary Messner, end Jim Temp, and Heisman Trophy winner Alan Ameche. Roll call ended with "Temp, Terry, Thomack, Todd, and Turnbull."

The inspection was progressing well, we thought, until the officer came upon Todd's bunk. Somehow, unnoticed, he had gone back into the barracks and, inexplicably, stuck a pair of tennis shoes under the blanket of his bunk. There went the weekend pass! Thereafter, I changed our roll call to "Temp, Terry, Thomack, TURD, and Toddbull."

> Lester asked his French friend, "What's the difference between an American rabbit and a French rabbit?"
>
> "Oh, merci," he quickly answered. "The American rabbit goes hippity-hop, and the French rabbit goes lickity-split."

My call to report for OCS was expected imminently, as I learned that the FBI had been around checking me out for secret security clearance. Shortly thereafter, I was notified to report in at Fort Eustis, Virginia, near Newport News, the shipbuilding center.

After only a few days, there was talk among the class about a woman spotted at the PX. I was seated next to Dominic Tarantino and, fortunately, hadn't repeated any of the talk I heard, as it was about his wife, Leonilda. Whether Dom caught any of this, I don't know, but I understood the stir when I met her. She wore size 3 shoes, her hands were just as small, and that's where the smallness ended. Leonilda was a very beautiful, blonde Italian girl.

The Tarantinos, from San Francisco, loved to entertain, and in time I would be a frequent dinner guest. She always served a frozen grapefruit salad.

I have no idea how he arranged it, but Dom was going to Washington, DC, to see the career management officer and asked if I'd care to go along. His purpose was to request assignment in Germany, and that's what I wanted too. The CMO listened to our request, made a note of it, and said he couldn't promise anything. Whether our attempt made any difference isn't known, but we did get assigned to Germany, and within the same division.

Circling Around

It was only a few weeks into OCS when my wife flew out from Wisconsin to join me in Washington, DC, for Easter weekend. I went back to Fort Eustis, and she flew home pregnant. Then I went back to Wisconsin after commissioning to bring her with me to Fort Dix, New Jersey, where I was to report for further orders.

We took a motel room, and I was to check in at the post every day to see if my orders had been cut. After the fourth day with no orders, we moved into a rooming house to save money. The fanciest thing about the furnishings was a bare light bulb that hung from a long cord.

Still no orders. The officer I was reporting to said he didn't know when the orders might be cut, but that I should take our Chevy Powerglide to Sand Point for shipment and then go back to Wisconsin until notified orders had been cut.

We took the car to the port and then boarded the Admiral train out of New York. We expected a comfortable ride, but the name belied the "comfort" we experienced. It was a miserable affair, as it was hot and the train had long stopovers at every little burg in Ohio. I used thirty days advance leave time before the call came.

My in-laws drove us back to Fort Dix. My father-in-law, George, took a big swig of his nerve medicine just before we entered the Holland Tunnel.

We flew out of LaGuardia on a commercial flight instead of a MATS flight. The plane was a Pan-American Constellation, the one with the triple vertical stabilizers, and our first stop was Gander, Newfoundland. Then it was on to Shannon, Ireland, before hopping over to the next stop, London Heathrow. The last leg was from London to Frankfurt Rhein-Main in Germany, where we were met by Sergeant Carter. He escorted us by train to Stuttgart, where he got us situated in the Steigenberger Graf Zeppelin hotel, a luxurious five-star establishment.

Sergeant Carter informed me I was to report the next morning to my company for a three-day field-training exercise. My wife was frightened to be left alone, and she said the maid found her in bed every morning because that's where she stayed for all three days before I returned.

I was assigned to the 444th Transportation Company, a light truck unit, and the company commander was Captain Jewell. The field trip was a tough start for me, as it's an experience you can't teach in the classroom, but I think I adjusted quite well and was the information and education officer for our group. The company was located in a former German army camp—or *kaserne* in the German vernacular—which was then named Ludendorff but has since changed to Badenerhof Kaserne. My driver was a heavy-footed Kentuckian, Corporal Jimes.

Janet and I were amazed at the housing we were assigned; we hadn't known what to expect. We had field-grade officers' quarters with the finest furniture, Rosenthal porcelain figurines, dinnerware, lead crystal glassware, and sterling silver flatware. It was complete and lacked nothing.

We hired a German maid, Erika, and she was very helpful in a number of ways, like getting us acquainted with the community and where to shop for anything in Heilbronn, which is about thirty-five miles from Stuttgart and was bombed twenty times by British and American forces. The city was the target of a revenge bombing when our American planes carpet-bombed it. Heilbronn is off-limits to all GIs on the anniversary date.

Geographically, we were perfectly located, as the cities of Heidelberg, Stuttgart, Augsburg, Munich, and Nuremburg were within easy driving distance. Unless on pass or leave, all military personnel were supposed to stay within fifty miles of their post. We loved the warmth and charm of the old cities, large and small, and on weekends there were always interesting festivals with roots going back hundreds of years.

Heilbronn seemed to be almost fully reconstructed, with little evidence, except an occasional pile of rubble, of the unimaginable destruction it suffered. In the Marketplatz, the main structure featured an astrological clock built in the sixteenth century, fully restored and operational. It was the biggest tourist attraction.

St. Kilian's Church was another great landmark and was believed to be standing on the site where St. Michael's Basilica stood and dated back to the year 741. Saint Kilian, a thirteenth-century saint, was first mentioned in a papal letter of indulgence in 1297. The church's reconstruction began in 1946 and was finished in 1974.

The military had a program called Operation Gyroscope, under which entire units were rotated back to the United States after a specified period of service overseas. Simultaneously, a fresh unit would be sent to replace the outgoing outfit. When the 444th's date for gyroscoping arrived, I was not yet eligible but did accompany them to the port, Bremerhaven, and escorted the incoming group to Heilbronn.

As we were pulling out of the kaserne, the frauleins were hanging all over the fences, screaming and crying as if it were the end of the world. When I returned with the new faces, the same frauleins were present and doing their best to attract new romantic interests. I would get reassigned to another light truck company in Neu Ulm, nearer Stuttgart and Ulm itself, the birthplace of Albert Einstein.

Janet and I became really good friends with another couple, Lou and Joanie Shapiro, he from Milwaukee and she from New York. Her father was president of Hiram Walker. She was the most unique individual we ever met, as she dared to ask any question, no matter how prying. We were totally shocked at first, but we took a great liking to her, as we found her to be completely honest and sincere herself. We entertained them a lot but don't remember ever being invited to their place.

Lou and Joanie visited Garmisch-Partenkirchen, the skiing mecca; became enthusiasts; and spent all their leisure time there. Lou must have found a way to manipulate the system, because they always seemed to have their weekends free for skiing. We never saw them again after.

Before this happened, we did take a trip with them to visit the Jewels of the Rhine, Lucerne and Zurich, and had the most wonderful time. Lucerne was the bigger tourist attraction, whereas Zurich featured luxurious shopping venues. Paris, Rome, and even London were popular destinations, but they just didn't appeal to us at the time. I know I'd still go back to Switzerland if it were a matter of choice today, and I would definitely spend more than a couple of days there this time.

Moving On

It was the dead of winter. The temperature had dropped to minus twenty-five degrees. No one was able to get his vehicle started, but my Chevy Powerglide fired up. Then I shifted to "reverse" to back out of my parking spot, and nothing happened. The car didn't move.

The mechanic I called came out and told me some part of the transmission had failed and needed to be replaced. Later, when I saw the part, it didn't make sense because there were no moving parts to wear out; it just had channels for fluid to pass through. I wondered if I'd been had. Could it have been that the transmission fluid was just low?

The mechanic ordered the part from the States. It would be shipped to Belgium and then to Ulm. Six weeks and $600 later, I was behind the wheel again.

The well-known St. Olaf College choir out of Minnesota was touring Germany, and we were able to go hear them when they were in Stuttgart. That was the first time we heard "The Little Drummer Boy."

My wife was pretty well along in her pregnancy, toward the end of December, when she thought the baby was coming. It was on a Sunday, and we drove to the hospital at Bad Connstatt, not far from Stuttgart. It turned out to be a false alarm, and we went home.

A couple of weeks later, again on a Sunday, she felt it was time, and we headed back to check into the hospital, where I took a place in the waiting room. Whenever the doctor appeared, I expected him to call my name, but over and over again the call was for someone else who had come in just shortly before.

Now it was late Monday afternoon, and I had to run back to Heilbronn to let our dog out. Duke was an oversized German shepherd I'd inherited from Sergeant Sanchez, who was part of the gyroscope move and couldn't keep him. When I got back to the hospital, still nothing had happened, and I went back to the waiting room, where I fell asleep until the doctor woke me Tuesday morning. Our daughter, all four pounds and fifteen ounces of her, had made her debut.

It was another week before we were able to take her home, because she had to weigh over five pounds first. Juliana was Queen of the Netherlands at the time, and we named our little princess Julie Anna—*Julie* for the queen and *Anna* for my mother. Erika, our maid, called the baby *Kleine Maus*—Little Mouse.

Julie Anna was about six weeks old when I took her and her mother to the airport in Stuttgart, where they flew out in a snowstorm to go back to the States. Janet was experiencing postpartum depression and thought she needed her mother more than me. Fourteen months later, we were reunited. Nine months after that, our first son was born.

Bachelor Officers' Quarters

With Janet's departure, I had to give up the officer's apartment and move into the bachelor officers' quarters, where I became friends with Chief Leon Carr. He ran the motor pool of my company. He was an "I don't give a damn" kind of guy, and it was apparent he was rather well acquainted with intoxicating liquids. Divorced and from Philadelphia, he told me many stories about his drinking escapades with his parish priest.

The company commander of my new unit was Captain Young, recently promoted and with his first command, but the sergeants were old hands and the mainstay of the company. My platoon sergeant was Herman Offield from Breckenridge, Texas. Sergeant Deal was another good one, and the company master sergeant, Mark Sykes, was a no-nonsense, all business, pleasant operator.

I was the company paymaster, and every month I'd work up the payroll, strap on my forty-five (which was never loaded), and pick up the payroll from the Quartermaster Corps. Back at the company, I'd break it down and distribute it. The system worked well.

Just as with my old company, there were troop field exercises of shorter duration. My drivers would drop them off in a designated area and draw back to a remote spot to wait for the signal to pick them up. One time, I had no idea where to find them, and we were forty-five minutes late by the time we did. Previously, I had found I could rely on my sergeants and driver to remember where the pickup point was, and I'd became lax in responsibility.

The next day, I was ordered to report to the division commander's office, and I figured I was really in trouble. Would I get demoted or what? The commander pointed out how serious this incident could have been in a different situation, and after the lecture, dismissed me on the condition it would never happen again. I gave him the snappiest salute and took my leave. Phew!

Sergeant Offield had taken me under his wing, and I went out with him and his fraulein a number of times to the local pubs. Cognac and Coke was the preferred drink for most of the women. Over the holidays, he invited me to join him and his girlfriend to spend an evening at her grandparents' house.

We were having a comfortable evening, drinking wine and enjoying the special holiday meal—after which Herman whispered to me that the old man would let me sleep with his wife if I'd let him smell my socks. Holy cow. What kind of fetish is that? I told him to tell Grandpa I was married and not interested.

Chief Carr had a gruff voice, and that belied the really nice man he was. He was good company, and we got along well. We took regular sightseeing jaunts, often stopping at one of the small local breweries to sample the wares, or we'd stop at a gasthaus for Wienerschnitzel as only the Germans can prepare it. It usually came with an egg sitting on it.

We ventured a little farther one weekend and went to the Bodensee, where we stayed at the Bodensee hotel and dined there. I'm not a big fan of fish, but I tried the Bodensee felchen and would give anything to have it again. It was of medium size and baked. The waitress opened the fish and, with two tiny forks, speedily removed the bones. Then she flipped it over and repeated the operation. The fish had a different texture, great flavor, and went well with my martini.

Chief had a 35mm Canon camera, and with one shot had a picture of the castle, statue, church, or whatever point of interest we were at. I had an 8mm movie camera, which was just not suited for the purpose, as I'd have to film for eight to ten seconds to cover the subject. I bought a German-made 35mm camera, an Iloca, and the pictures were every bit as good or better than Chief's Canon produced.

I was a little leery of the film transport, as it didn't seem solid, so I sold the Iloca and bought a Retina in case I needed service in the future. I checked to see if the Iloca is still available and found I should have bought a Hasselblad, as it's only $47,995; twelve easy monthly payments of $4,000 is the offer.

There was a local camera shop, from which I rented a projector to view my slides. The projector was a Lisagang, and it would fill an entire wall from a few feet, while the Kodak Carousel I purchased at home put up a much smaller picture even from farther away.

My favorite restaurant in Ulm was in the Ulmer Muenster hotel, which was only a few steps from the Ulm Cathedral. The cathedral is the highest stone structure in the world, and the steeple is the tallest. Visitors can climb the 762 steps to the top, and I did it. Magnificent views from up there. The cathedral itself is a wonder and filled with wooden figures carved by artisans who spent their entire lives on the project. Inside, it's like standing in a forest.

Chief wasn't familiar with Ulmer Muenster, but my wife and I were, having dined there regularly and always choosing the three-item special, which consisted of a cutlet, steak, and whole squab or quail with the head on and the eyeball peering up at you. As usual, the steak was topped with an egg. Chief couldn't believe he hadn't heard about the place.

Another restaurant my wife and I favored was the Drei Kannen, also in Ulm. It was well worth going there just for the oxtail soup, but overall it served excellent food.

CHAPTER 11

And Back to Civilian Life

I was nearing the end of my active-duty days. I was considering extending my time and wrote my wife accordingly. She answered that I could do that and have a divorce, or come home and have a family. Actually, it was a moot consideration, because when I inquired about it, I learned the military was being cut back so extending wasn't a possibility.

My flight home was at night out of Frankfurt and was again on a Pan-American Constellation. My assigned seat was a window seat at the rear of the plane. We were on the ground for a long time with the engines running when I noticed red hot embers falling from the engine pods. I thought the glowing things were engine parts and called the stewardess to alert her. She explained those were just carbon particles being burned off and not a concern.

The flight itself wasn't remarkable, except I could feel the tail of the plane move from side to side in the buffeting winds.

It wasn't long after I returned home that I found out my mother-in-law was aghast when told our daughter had been baptized in the Lutheran Church—which was what my wife had wanted too—and prevailed upon my wife to have Julie Anna rebaptized in the Catholic Church. That was only the beginning of the influence and interference we were to experience with her.

Shortly after I got home, the in-laws insisted on having my parents come over to their house for what turned out to be an inquiry into our financial affairs. Why didn't I have as much money when I got out of the service as their friend's daughter Charlene's husband had? Now, I don't know how she could have known anything about our financial matters unless she got it out of my wife, who really didn't know herself.

About the nicest thing I could say about my mother-in-law was that she always wore her long hair in a French Twist and was quite attractive, despite her big honker, with which she was well equipped to go about her snooping. Charlene's husband was an enlisted man who didn't drink or smoke and saved all his pay. He had no expenses, as his housing and meals were provided. When I moved into the bachelor officers' quarters, I had that expense, plus I had to pay for all my meals at the Officers' Club. I also had car expenses in addition to the car payment itself, and I was still paying off the cost of my wife's airfare home. And of course, I didn't spend all my off-duty time just sitting in my quarters.

I never should have agreed to having my parents summoned and subjected to this invasion of our privacy. It reminded me of the first time my future mother-in-law met my mother, as I noticed she was trying to see down my mother's dress to tell if she was wearing clean underwear.

One day out of the clear blue, my mother-in-law asked if I knew who was the first martyr of the church, and she seemed surprised when I told her it was Stephen. She knew I went to a parochial school, so what did she think we were taught?

Marathon Corporation

My first job was with Marathon Corporation, where I'd worked in the research lab after high school and as a pressman's helper just before going into the military. The job was in the Washington Street plant, also known as the carton plant, versus the River Street plant, which was the film plant. The job entailed calculating incentive pay for the tool and die makers.

Measurements were made of the given carton's perimeter along with the length of the scores, cut-scores, or perforations in the body. Each result was multiplied by a factor and the results passed on to the paymaster, which was my next job. The payroll covered about six hundred plant employees, from pressmen to maintenance people and janitors. In addition, another hundred and fifty workers from the woodlands operation and over-the-road truck drivers were part of the same payroll. It was both a satisfying and rather frustrating job, because as soon as you completed the current weekly payroll, you had to jump into the next one with no break at all. The worst part of it was that the janitor made more money than I did.

During an audit by an outside firm, two of the auditors asked me to make a calculation on a *comptometer*, a mechanical calculator. I did as asked, and the auditors looked at each other, kind of bewildered. I guess they weren't familiar with the machine and asked me to redo the calculation, for which I came up with the same answer. They kind of smiled, shook their heads, and walked away.

Janet and I moved from one apartment to another and then to a duplex before buying our first home, a hundred-year-old former farmhouse. The place had been modernized, and one of the five bedrooms had been converted to a mother-in-law's quarters complete with a kitchen and bath. It served as the nursery for our third child. The master bedroom was walled with built-ins, and the house had a great country kitchen with three bread boards.

The foundation walls were three feet thick and stone and kept cold year round, so we didn't need air-conditioning; the fan circulated the cool air throughout the entire house. The old monster furnace was equipped with an automatic coal feeder. Initially, the in-laws were completely opposed to our buying the place, but we were happy with the house and, for some reason, all the family gatherings were held there.

It was only a short time after the audit that I took a transfer to the cost accounting department in the River Street plant on the other side of the Fox River. The plants were connected by an enclosed walkway over the river. The job entailed working up standard product costs developed from product specifications prepared by the time-study engineers.

About half of our department employees were women. Breaks were taken departmentally, and during one midmorning break, Jack Jablonski, a new and young employee, asked if everyone had heard about the terrible car accident that had happened the night before. "Isn't it terrible? Did you hear the guy was castrated?"

The girls split, like right now.

The remaining men asked Jack, "Do you know what *castration* is?"

Jack said, "Yeah, that's when your head is cut off."

"No, Jack, that's *decapitation*. Castration is when …"

It was hard to convince Jack to come back to face the women after the break.

Bob Marsh was the head accountant under the plant accountant, Dutch Liebelt, who I thought was very odd and noncommunicative. At any rate, Marsh would just agonize every month-end when he had to compile all the month's data to prepare a departmental statement. His stomach would be in a knot as he struggled with it until it was completed. Normally, he was an easygoing, carefree person, and always joking, so the pressure of the job can get to you.

Marathon Corporation had merged with American Can Company and was building a plant in Louisville, Kentucky, specifically to better service the cigarette industry, become more competitive, and improve the profitability of the business. I was offered the job as plant accountant.

Before I move on here, I want to tell about another situation. The brother of one of my coworkers raised corn-fed Black Angus cattle, and I bought a half at a time. That's a lot of meat. Fantastic meat. I had a butcher cut it up and freeze-wrap it for storage in a rented locker, as we didn't have a freezer at home, at least not one to accommodate so much volume. Once a week, I'd go to the freezer to bring home what my wife ordered.

One day, my mother-in-law cornered me and asked why I only fed hamburger to my family. Our hamburger was gone well before the rest of the cuts, but it was top grade, versatile, and what the wife preferred. How my mother-in-law made this her business is beyond me, except she must have had a discussion about our menus with my wife. It was none of her dang business, and I should have told her to keep her big schnoz out of our affairs. My wife made great dishes with the ground beef and meat roasts, while I normally fixed the steaks.

Transplanted

Uprooting your family, leaving friends and relatives, and moving to a new location isn't an easy choice, and it was several days before we decided we wanted to go ahead with the move. One of my personal motives was to get my wife away from the outlaws … I mean in-laws. I'm not saying they were bad people by any means, but my mother-in-law knew everybody's business as to who did this or who did that or who was gay, and my father-in-law thought anybody who didn't agree with him was a fathead. Somehow,

I didn't feel any sympathy for him when he was circumcised at about the age of fifty ... just an afterthought here.

Horace Dicke was going to be my new boss, and the rest of the original crew transferring to Louisville consisted of the three pressmen to act as shift supervisors, a color matcher who was Horace's buddy (both were outstanding bowlers), and another fellow to serve as the production scheduler. Three weeks of supervisory training preceded our actual move, plus there were frequent staff meetings, usually evening affairs. The presenter of the training series was King Evans out of our New York offices, and the overall theme was attitude, or *at-tee-tude*, as King pronounced the word.

I was never a nervous person or a worrier for that matter, but the anticipation of the new position was wearing on me. The prospect of a new job with no one to train me and so many unknowns was starting to get to me. I would take crème de menthe to calm my stomach. It reached the point where my stools were just as green as the aperitif I was consuming.

I had such doubts about being able to cope with the situation, and I recalled what the pressure did to Bob Marsh. I thought I had to tell Horace that I doubted my ability to do the job. Up until then, I had only known him as a member of the church I attended. I'm sure I caused him a good bit of consternation when I talked to him. He must have wondered about his choice. He assured me he had complete confidence in me and that I would manage just fine.

Jack, the color matcher, and I drove to Louisville for a preliminary visit, but I don't remember the purpose for it. He had a tiny Skoda, a Czechoslovakian-made vehicle. It was so small and uncomfortable, it was like riding an ironing board. Jack was a tall fellow, and his knees were higher than the dashboard when he was behind the wheel.

The company allowed us three days to house hunt, and Janet and I flew out on a DC-3 with Leroy, the production scheduler, and his wife, Janell, who was a mousy whisperer. I don't like to judge people, but first impressions are often quite indicative of a person's true nature. It was the second day when we found a three-bedroom, two-bath brick ranch on Glen Oak Drive, a cul-de-sac, and we were able to assume the mortgage of the current owners because the interest rate on the mortgage was below the current rate for new mortgages, plus we were able to avoid the usual closing costs and title search fee. We tried to duplicate this in time back in Wisconsin but state law there didn't allow it. That was too bad, because mortgage rates were 16 percent or higher at the time.

That evening, we decided to go to the bar at the Holiday Inn where we were staying to have a celebratory drink. We sat at the bar but were told women weren't permitted to do that in Kentucky under the Blue Law, so we took our seat at a table.

Another time, I left money on the bar next to my drink. When I got up to go to the men's room, the bartender called me back to tell me I should pick up the money. He didn't explain why I shouldn't leave it there. It was never a problem in Wisconsin.

Leroy and Janell found a place not too far from our house, and that was good because Leroy and I were able to alternate driving in our commute to the plant, which about seven miles distant.

> The girl behind the counter watched as the old man struggled to get to the bar, and with some effort managed to get onto the stool, at which time he let out a big sigh of relief. She studied him for a few seconds before asking him what he was having. "I'd like a hot fudge sundae," he replied.

"Crushed nuts?" inquired the girl.

"No, ah … rheumatism," he grunted.

After taking my wife back to Wisconsin, since our new house wouldn't be ready for occupancy for another month, I had to report for work and flew back to Louisville. The plant was still under construction, but the production portion was already completed, and the machinery was in shakedown mode with new-employee training taking place simultaneously. I was met at the airport and escorted to the plant to prepare the initial payroll, as the workers had been on the job for two weeks without a paycheck.

The office area wasn't completed, and there was no furniture. An improvised desk was made of a sheet of drywall spanning a couple stacks of cement blocks. Cement blocks also served as my office chair.

Horace showed some consideration for decision-making by those who would occupy the offices by allowing us to choose the paneling we preferred. My choice was cherry, which resulted in a rich, warm sanctuary for me. My office was the only one with direct access to the production area and the main office. Leroy's was adjacent to Horace's, and Jack's was situated out in the plant section, as was that of the production supervisors.

Initially, we started the operation with a skeleton staff, but all the aspects of regular business had to be attended to, and that's how I got assigned purchasing and personnel in addition to my primary duties as the plant accountant. I had to build an operating budget and prepare pro forma statements, neither of which I'd done before. The budget contained fixed and variable elements; fixed costs didn't change, but the variable items did according to production levels. Also, I had to build standard product cost schedules for the various products, for which I did have some prior experience. The process was relatively simple until we got into flexible packaging.

At the outset, our primary jobs were for Marlboro flip-top boxes and master carton. The manufacturing process was an in-line operation, where the printed stock came off the press into a stamping machine, which actually cut out the cartons, stripped away the trim portion, and shingled them onto a conveyor from which they were stacked on pallets.

There weren't enough hours in a normal workday for me to complete all my work, and consequently, I worked long hours into the evenings for the first eight or nine months. When the plant went into round-the-clock production, I often saw all three production supervisors, including the third-shift guy at 11 p.m. As a result, I lost so much weight I had to rely on suspenders to hold my trousers up.

Horace appointed me as information and ezducation (I&E) officer too. That entailed making presentations at our monthly staff dinner meetings. I put special effort into choosing subject matter and tried to make them as interesting as I could, because I understood that just reporting operating results wasn't going to hold everyone's attention. But I never got any show of appreciation from Horace, who didn't understand what the undertaking involved. He did say in my one and only annual review that I had to learn to blow my own horn, to which I replied I just let my performance speak for me.

It was after one of these meetings that Leroy and I were having a cocktail together annd he told me he and Horace were mustangs. When I asked what *mustangs* were, he said they were guys who made it without a college education. That explained a lot to me about their conduct. Leroy did all he could to suck up to Horace, and nobody could not notice it.

By now, we had a payroll clerk, and Jack was doing all the plant hiring. The purchasing I did didn't include production materials, such as paperboard stock, label paper stock, and inks, so I had some relief there, but the company introduced a profit improvement program, and I was named to manage it. Anyone could suggest a savings project and the committee would review it for compliance with the requirements to be a viable undertaking. It had to be a current expense, measureable, and so on, and it could be either a one-shot or ongoing. If I deemed an idea acceptable, I had to write it up, calculate the savings, and report actual savings in subsequent meetings. It proved to be a worthwhile program.

Business was growing, and we expanded into the soft packaging and cup labels for cigarettes with the addition of another Champlain rotogravure press, slitters to cut jumbo rolls into single rolls, and a rewinder. Standard cost estimating was much more complicated here, and cost estimates were key tools for the basis of negotiating contracts with the cigarette companies. These were expressed down to 1/10,000 of a cent, as the contracts involved quantities in excess of 250 million, so it was important to be that accurate.

I won't go into the cost elements, but having a good rapport with the production staff was truly helpful. Paul Morgan, a national sales manager and full of himself, with a Sherlock Homes–style pipe hanging from his mouth, always came in for the negotiations.

Leroy got an assistant, then a different one after another, until he'd had at least twelve come and go during the six-year period I was there. I have no idea what drove them off except Leroy had a bias toward college graduates, and when Matt Klusmeier announced he had gotten his master's degree, Leroy said to me in an aside, "Yah, Klusmeier just got his bastard's degree." Another of Leroy's casualties was Don Goben, a truly nice guy and a Kenny Rogers lookalike.

Horace had a similar problem. One day, he was on his way to the airport when I realized a report I needed was in his office.

His secretary was very reluctant to open his office but relented. She was at his desk looking for the document, and I was standing back from it, when Horace appeared, as he had come back for something he forgot. I can only imagine what he put that poor girl through for allowing somebody into his sanctuary without his being there. If Leroy went through twelve assistants, Horace had at least six different secretaries during the same period.

Horace admitted to me once that he was suspicious and only wished he were twice as suspicious. He proved his suspicious nature in another way when I had the staff at my house after a dinner meeting. I had a bedroom and a recreation room with a serviceable bar built in my basement using hickory paneling. My wife was entertaining the women upstairs. It was then that Horace accused me in front of everybody of keeping two sets of books, and he was serious. He asked how else my cost estimates could be so close to actual.

That completely changed the tone of our social hour. The supervisors told me they weren't the least bit surprised, because they used to catch Horace spying on them back at the old plant.

Horace liked his whiskey, and he was in my neighborhood bar one time when I stopped for a beverage on the way home.

"Bob," he asked, "why don't we bury the hatchet?"

I said, "Horace, I don't know what you're talking about. I don't have an axe to grind with you."

He said, "Oh, for God's sake!" and stalked off. I wondered if that came from Leroy.

An accountants' conference was scheduled in Chicago, for which I flew out of Louisville on a Lockheed Electra turboprop plane. Shortly after takeoff, we heard a big bang at the rear of the plane. The captain came on and announced, "There was an unaccounted-for loud bang at the rear of the plane, and we'll be returning to Standiford Field to check it out."

The passenger sitting next to me said, "Oh boy. They'll deplane us and break out the champagne."

The plane circled around as it dumped fuel before we landed. We were not deplaned. Instead, they brought out a big acetylene tank and started welding while we were aboard. After a delay, the captain declared that we were cleared for departure and would make up the lost time so we'd still get into Chicago near scheduled arrival time Those were words I didn't want to hear, because Lockheed Electras had been restricted to a maximum speed after several accidents when the wings broke off.

Sterling Forest Presentation

The management staff was notified of an upcoming meeting by a group from corporate called the Sterling Forest Presentation. Quickly getting to the gist of the meeting, the moderator informed us that the company was going to be distributing money to exempt employees. After explaining the program, he said he would entertain questions about it. Nobody responded.

He looked us over and threw up his hands. "What? Nobody has a question? We're talking about a lot of money here, and nobody has a question?"

Still no response. The reason there weren't any questions was because Horace was sitting there with his watchful eye. No one wanted to risk his look of disapproval.

The moderator kind of shook his head and told us, "You are the strangest group of people I've ever met."

No one would have guessed the distribution would be at the discretion of our leader, as we were expecting the money would be allocated according to actual salaries and that would have led to a fair share. Horace deemed my share to be all of thirteen dollars. A person at corporate, probably known to me but not wanting to be identified, secreted a copy of the distribution to me, unknown to Horace. The moderator was correct when he said he was talking about a lot of money, and I don't have to tell you who got his "fair" share.

During the previous basketball season, a vice president out of corporate had paid us a visit. He came into my office, and we had a very pleasant conversation. He was a huge Kentucky Wildcats fan and attended a number of games each year. He leaned forward and in a very confidential tone said, "Bob, if you ever need anything, be sure to contact me." I wondered, did he sense something strange about what he witnessed?

Well, the time had come after Sterling Forest, and I did send him a note saying I was in a situation I wanted to discuss or make him aware of. But he never answered. Perhaps he would have if it had been during basketball season and he could justify a visit. Now there wasn't a question in my mind about what I was going to do.

The first time I checked the Louisville *Courier Journal*'s want ad section, I found one for a controller position in Wisconsin. I inquired about it and was interviewed by Gordon Stewart, the corporate controller at Thomas Industries. I was given a test, largely math stuff, which I knew I had aced. When I accepted the offer extended, Gordon cautioned me thusly: "American Can is going to counteroffer to try to keep you."

I assured him I was committed and for him not to be concerned. He would later introduce me as "the best cost accountant in the Midwest."

In my letter of resignation, I wasn't going to say the usual stuff. I expressed regret, as I always deemed myself to be a loyal employee, and then cited the intolerable atmosphere that existed while also mentioning the constant employee turnover. It was on a Friday when I mailed a copy of it to New York and put the letter in Horace's inbox.

He came in a little late the following Monday. It didn't take long for Horace to react, and that was to consult with Leroy, who thought every attempt at a joke by Horace was a knee-slapper. The office door slammed shut. It wasn't long before Barb, Horace's secretary, called me to say, "Mr. Dicke would like you to come to his office."

Horace got right to the point. "Bob, you've got so much talent. Won't you please reconsider resigning?"

I thought to myself, *Yeah, you really acknowledged my talent when you saw fit to reward me with those thirteen dollars of Sterling Forest allocation.* I told Horace changing my mind wasn't a possibility, as I had mailed the resignation to corporate, which precluded any other option. We never spoke again, even after I stayed on after the two-week notice period had passed.

I called Mr. Stewart to get permission to stay an additional week because of the circumstances. I didn't feel good about walking away with no prospect for a replacement. It wasn't that I owed anybody, particularly Horace. Maybe it was a carryover of company loyalty, plus I could leave in good conscience. Mr. Stewart said he expected that of me.

There wasn't a lack of candidates, but none showed any interest in further consideration after seeing what all the position entailed. One prospect was an accountant, Ralph Kober, from the team I worked with back in Wisconsin. Ralph didn't want anything to do with the job and left for the airport.

When Horace heard this, he raced to the airport to intercept Ralph and try to stop him from leaving. Ralph politely told him what he could do with the job.

One of the last candidates to come in before I left was a CPA from the Indianapolis location. We spent two and a half days together before he departed too, but he thanked me for giving him a better understanding of standard cost accounting, which he hadn't fully grasped when studying it in college. That was Terrance Windsor, and he declined further consideration.

Actually, I don't know how long it was before someone was

hired or if they broke up the job to make it less forebidding, but I did hear that Horace was removed shortly thereafter and given a menial job in quality control back at the old Wisconsin plant he came from. He only stayed until he found an unknown position at Kimberly-Clark Corporation in Neenah.

My wife and I really loved living in Louisville. We had a nice home, great neighbors, restaurants, etc. However, we were not happy with the Kentucky School for the Blind, which my visually impaired son was attending. We and others didn't think it was much more than a glorified day care operation, and coming back to Wisconsin was important to us for that reason.

Derby Day

The Kentucky Derby horse race is always run on the first Saturday in May, and 1963 was our first opportunity to attend, which we did as guests of the local bank we dealt with. We had perfect seats that were about five rows back from the track and right where the horses come out from the paddock, where they are saddled up and paraded before the races. Interestingly, the horses race by the grandstand only once on Derby Day, and that's for the Derby itself.

We knew nothing about the horses, but I had heard an employee at work mention a horse named Chateaugay, so I picked him, as did my father-in-law, who was there for the Derby. Chateaugay was a chestnut, my favorite in horses, and went off at 15–1, as I recall, so not a favorite at the betting window. He was far, far back of the field when he started his charge, overtook the field, and won the race.

Two weeks later at the Preakness, he had a repeat performance, again coming from way back of the field to win and have a chance to be a Triple Crown winner. But the strategy didn't work for the mile and a half Belmont Stakes three weeks later. He will always remain my favorite pony.

Chateaugay was the son of Swaps, the horse that beat Nashua in the famous 1955 Derby. Swaps, also a chestnut, was named Horse of the Year and a Hall of Fame inductee. He lost just four times in thirty outings.

On the Road

After the Chevrolet Powerglide, I drove nothing but Buicks except for the 1965 Ford, which was my first brand new car. The first Buick I owned was a 1959 chrome-laden Buick Special, and I always had it serviced before taking a trip.

Now it was November 1963, and we were heading back to Wisconsin for Thanksgiving. We had made it to Indianapolis when my gas gauge showed nearly empty after only about 110 miles, when I usually needed to gas up just once for the 450-mile distance. I didn't have any idea what was wrong, as I had just got the car from the service garage—but I had to fill up again after another hundred miles. The third stop was just before Chicago, and that's where we heard that Kennedy had been shot. My radio was out, so we didn't know he died until we got to our destination, Neenah.

Of course, I experienced the same rate of gas consumption on the return trip and went back to my mechanic to find out what was the problem. I knew nothing about engines, but he said the heat riser valve was broken, and that is why the usage never abated. It wasn't broken when I took it in, so it must have happened in the garage.

After taking over eleven hours to make the 450-mile drive home and eleven hours to make the return trip, we started to pack sandwiches to eat on the road and also packed an empty peanut butter jar as a portable potty, which eliminated the need to make rest stops, cutting our driving time by almost four hours.

The tollway around Chicago must not have been completed yet, as we took Highway 41 to Evanston and then the Ryan Expressway through Chicago. I continued to do that even when the toll roads were done. Heading home after Thanksgiving and just outside of Evanston, we found police officers standing in the middle of the highway, and they waved us off the road onto the shoulder with instructions to wait there until an officer came. Strangely, only cars with out-of-state plates were pulled over.

I was led to a policeman's site of some kind and had to pay a ninety dollar "fine" to get released. It was about two weeks later that I received a refund check for the full amount without an explanation. I think they pulled over the wrong vehicle and the driver was able to expose the shenanigans.

Meanwhile, I had to gas up again and stopped at a Texaco station in Gary, Indiana, to fill up. The Evanston police had all my cash, so I was going to use my gas credit card, but the attendant wouldn't accept it, even though it was for Texaco. The attendant impounded my car with my wife and our three kids.

There was a Big Boy restaurant a few hundred yards away, and I walked there looking for help. A gentleman overheard me explaining my predicament. He came over and handed me $100. He happened to own a Big Boy in Louisville, the one I frequented. He didn't ask for identification, collateral, or anything—just outright gave me the money, no questions asked. Wow!

The next day was Monday, and immediately after my bank opened, I went to pay back the gift and was never so happy to repay a good Samaritan.

Before leaving the Kentucky scene, I want to tell about the auto accident I had. Traffic on the bypass was always crowded, and it was common to come to complete stops. I had just recently purchased my first brand-new car. It was stop and go, stop and go, when at a complete stop I looked at the rearview mirror and saw the vehicle behind me wasn't going to stop. I braced myself as the loaded county gravel truck slammed into my car, driving the trunk deck all the way up to the back window.

I got out of my vehicle and fell to my knees. I have no recollection of how I got home. The next day, I visited a chiropractor and found that several of my vertebrae had been twisted ninety degrees. Little did I know I'd have ongoing issues from then on and need adjustments whenever I got out of sorts.

The following week, I had an unannounced visitor. I walked out to see him with a big brace on my neck and my head cocked to the side. I didn't have the presence of mind to take his card, so I didn't know if he was a lawyer for the county or its insurance agent, but he asked what I wanted and I foolishly said, "Just cover my medical and car repair expenses." Hard telling how big of a settlement I might have received, but it wasn't long after my accident that I had jury duty and heard that in anothing pcase, a woman who just got tapped in the rear end at a stop sign was awarded $50,000, a nice sum back in 1965.

The only case I served jury duty for was about a Black woman who was injured when she fell into an unmarked excavation one night. She incurred medical expenses and had a lengthy recovery period. The evidence showed the contractor failed to put up barricades and was clearly at fault. The first vote was unanimous in favor of the plaintiff, and the recommendation was to award the woman the tidy sum of one dollar. That was just outrageous, and I protested until we agreed on a settlement to pay her medical expenses plus $10,000.

Moving On

Our house on Glenn Oak Drive sold quickly, so we didn't have a concern there except we liked the place so much and couldn't have had better neighbors. Dr. Gerald Sasser lived on one side of us and Bob and Margaret Walker on the other. Rita and Howard Bowles were next to the Walkers. Dr. Sasser, a general practitioner, moved, and a younger couple, Mike and Sarah Moreland, bought the place.

One evening, Mike and Sarah attended a movie at a theater in downtown Louisville and parked their new Ford convertible on the street in front of the theater. When they came out, they found their car propped up on cement blocks with all the wheels missing. There seemed to be a market for wheels and tires, because this kind of thievery was common.

Bob Walker was a salesman for Carter, a children's clothing manufacturer, and he traveled a lot of the time. The Walkers were big-time Louisville Cardinal basketball fans, and Margaret loved to say Wes Unseld, the current star, "wasn't a N …, he was just a nice colored boy," and she'd laugh. Not nice, Margaret!

Wes went on to star in the NBA and coached the Washington Wizards. Margaret did grow the best roses along the back of their house—Queen Elizabeth, American Beauty, and Peace among them.

Rita talked about "Hard."

I asked, "Who's Hard?"

She said, "Hard, Hard, my husband."

Oh, that would be *Howard*, who was a claims adjuster for an insurance company while taking evening courses at the University of Louisville to become a lawyer. He finished his studies and set up an office downtown with Rita as his secretary until business was good enough to afford to hire one.

The Bowles's had five children. Howard liked his "bald" pota-toes and took his car in for "all" changes. Translation: *boiled* and *oil*. Now we didn't think we had an accent, but they said we did: a New York accent.

Our visually impaired son was three years old when we moved to Kentucky, so we were thankful to have found a place on a cul-de-sac. Our Scott would go from door to door, climbing up on the stoops. He might have been five when Rita told my wife how cute it was when Scott came to her door and asked for a cookie. I told Scott he shouldn't do that because it was bad manners, but it was OK if someone offers you a treat.

The next day, Scott was back at Rita's door, saying, "Mrs. Bowles, you wouldn't want to offer me a cookie, would you?"

To my ongoing dismay, Janet continued to have garage sales with ridiculous prices on the articles, such as twenty-five cents for a Ship 'N Shore blouse or two dollars for a cashmere sweater. Our kids never had hand-me-downs, but she did keep the baby crib and christening gown. Each pregnancy required a new wardrobe.

Our younger son, John, had heard us talk so favorably about our Kentucky neighbors, especially the Bowleses, that he decided to call on them when on a business trip there. He also wanted to see the house we lived in when he was born. He was only a year old when we moved, so Rita had no idea who the young man at her door might be. John introduced himself, and as they were talking, Howard walked through the living room attired in his birthday suit. Sad.

Back to Badger Land

It was departure time for me, and I flew into Milwaukee's Mitchell International Airport. Gordon Stewart had arranged for someone, I don't remember his name (perhaps one's subconscious mind blocks out unpleasant things), to pick me up and drive me to Sheboygan, some sixty miles away. The guy was completely un-communicative, only answering a question with a grunt or curt response, so it wasn't a pleasant ride. I did get to understand his antipathy when I learned I was the replacement for his best friend, who had been fired. I never saw or heard of him again, so it's likely he quit the company.

The Sheboygan location was called the Power Air Division, formerly Wright Saw. The primary product was fractional horsepower compressors, and the biggest customers were Xerox, Sears, and the US government. Sears demanded to audit the books and screwed prices down so low it wasn't a practical business. Paperwork made the government business hard to deal with, and again, it wasn't very profitable. Xerox was great and gave Thomas its Quality Vendor flag award. The fractional horsepower compressors were also in heavy demand in the medical field. Portable paint sprayers made up another product line, but Wright Saw was gone by now.

The announcement with my picture in the *Sheboygan Press* stated, "Thomack, a Neenah native, will be responsible for general accounting, cost accounting, credit and collection, billing, payroll, internal reporting, and budgeting for the division."

The housing market in Sheboygan was very tight, with virtually no established houses for sale, but I found a spec house for which I made an offer. It was a split-level in a new development. I really didn't like the house or the location and asked for a release from the contract when I found another house under construction and nearer completion. The realtor, a lawyer who was married into one of the wealthiest families, readily consented and returned my earnest down payment.

I was still able to make some changes in the four-bedroom two-bath house with different outside brick treatment and front windows, stainless steel instead of ceramic kitchen sinks, lannon stone instead of brick fireplace facing, and an added patio off the family room. The changes increased the price of the house by 10 percent. It was finished just in time for us to move in, as we had to give up occupancy of our Kentucky home.

The first new neighbors we got acquainted with lived across

the street from us, and the street hadn't been paved yet. Reuben was a small humpbacked man but a hell of a nice guy, and we became really good friends as we golfed and played cribbage together. Reuben answered the phone, "Sonnefeld's summer home. Some are home, and some are not."

Mrs. Sonnenfeld, Arlene, was quite nice too, but I had a little problem with her. She worked as a checkout clerk at a nearby Piggly Wiggly, made good money as a member of the Meat Cutters' Union, but drove a turd-beater that any self-respecting redneck would disown. When Arlene came home from work, she'd make a U-turn and park that heap in front of our house. Not very neighborly, and this continued until Reuben got a different car.

Before that, Reuben said he'd never buy a Japanese television set, but he bought one the day after he saw the great picture on our Panasonic set. He was getting nothing but a snowstorm on his Zenith.

Reuben and I went to a Wisconsin football game in Madison and left early enough to have time to play a round of golf at Windsor's Country Club in Sun Prairie just outside of Madison. We drove in my Buick Electra, easily the nicest and most comfortable vehicle I owned up to that point.

Well, a week later, Reuben was driving a Buick Electra, and Arlene moved up to his old car, a lesser Buick. Reuben, a huge Green Bay Packers fan, sported a bumper sticker on his new wheels that said "Packer Assistant Coach."

Sin City

Sheboygan, located equidistant from Milwaukee and Green Bay on the western shore of Lake Michigan, was often referred to as Sin City because at one time there were forty houses of ill repute in the immediate area. Well-known among them were the Ace of

Clubs, the Airport Inn, the Big Apple, the Brown House, and the Nightingale, which was nicknamed the Gonorrhea Racetrack by locals but later was renamed the Dreamland Ballroom. Then there was the Greenhouse, most popular and owned by Hatti Cook.

Besides the local patrons, sailors made Sheboygan a popular layover stop, as its reputation was widespread. However, the situation began to change after a Minneapolis newspaper ran an exposé about the booming business and generated too much bad publicity. Then most doors were shuttered, and businesses closed in early 1951 when twenty-four agents from the state beverage tax division raided six of the brothels on the same day, charging keepers and owners with delinquent beverage taxes. Hatti Cook alone was charged $100,000 plus interest on unpaid liquor taxes, over a million dollars in today's money. Other establishments also incurred very high charges, and the result was the end of the brothel era.

After shedding the brothel capital designation, Sheboygan became known more suitably as the City of Four Cs: chairs, cheese, children, and churches. At the time, there were twelve furniture companies in business locally. Currently, a fifth C could be added for the charter fishing boats, a business that blossomed after the state Department of Natural Resources planted coho and Chinook salmon in Lake Michigan.

Sheboygan is recognized in other ways, too. It is known as the Bratwurst Capital of the World, Malibu of the Midwest, and also the Freshwater Surf Capital of the World. Local yokels often fail to recognize or appreciate the great assets in their own community. Sheboygan, for some instances, offers the following:

❖ Mead Public Library, a three-story edifice with over 330,000 items and over 900,000 users annually
❖ Stefanie H. Weill Center for the Performing Arts, featuring the most famous entertainers from Hollywood

and New York at times. It is on the National Register of Historic Sites. In 1996, a preservation and restoration program began, which over a five-year period cost 5 million dollars.

❖ Blue Harbor Resort and Convention Center, with 224 rooms, suites, villas, five restaurants, and an indoor water park

❖ over a hundred restaurants and supper clubs in the county area

❖ an extensive park system

❖ John Michael Kohler Center for Performing Arts

❖ five-star American Club in nearby Kohler

❖ International airport

❖ eighteen golf courses in the area, including Whistling Straights, host of the PGA's US Open and Ryder Cup competition, and Pine Hills Country Club, an excellent private club

❖ Great Lakes salmon fishing

❖ mile-long beach, surfing, parasailing and kite surfing

❖ riverfront with shops, restaurants, charter boats, and fine condos

❖ beautiful harbor with two lighthouses and a yacht club

❖ Above and Beyond Children's Museum

All in all, Sheboygan offered a broad range of options for recreational, cultural, and entertainment venues.

Charlie

The line of authority was never clearly defined, and this was a source of frustration for me at times. We had a headstrong plant manager, Charles Holmes, who was quite new in the position, as the previous manager had been fired along with the controller. Charlie didn't see eye-to-eye on certain issues with Roger Dugan, the director of sales and engineering, so it was a classic power struggle between them. There was a lot of static in what communication they did have.

Now, Charles had an affected Southern accent. He wasn't Charlie, he was "Chalie." Well, perhaps it wasn't affected. After all, he did come from Fort Atkinson in southern Wisconsin.

Charlie would do things behind my back, like pull cash receipts from the current month to cover a shortage from the prior month's total, and he was doing that month after month. I suggested he take a hit for a month and then he wouldn't have to keep up the sham, because we'd be on an even keel thereafter. The girls in credit and collection were ordered to desist by me but then were overpowered by Holmes, so they were in a constant quandary.

Charlie usually called me into his office before a staff or production meeting to go over issues and get my reaction or opinions. During the actual meetings, he'd voice my thoughts and suggestions as though they were originally his, without acknowledging that he'd picked my brain for them. Yes, Charlie only saw himself—another Bonaparte.

Charlie and I attended a three-day conference in Chicago along with Dennis Hartman, our production manager. We stayed at the Drake Hotel, so we were within walking distance of a lot of restaurants. Dennis got to choose where to go on the first evening and opted for a Polynesian, which turned out to be a good choice. My choice for the next evening was Benihana West, and when we arrived, Dennis and I visited the men's room briefly.

Dennis and I looked at each other in disbelief when Charlie announced, "Ah ordered for us." Just how presumptive can a person become? Well, fortunately for Charlie, Dennis and I were quite pleased with the entrée and wine selected.

During the three days in Chicago, we heard Charlie rave over and over again about the chocolate mousse served at the restaurant in the hotel he once stayed at. As the hotel was too far to walk to, we got there by taxi cab—only to discover chocolate mousse was not being offered that evening. Somehow, Dennis and I didn't mind at all.

The three of us were to attend another three-day seminar at the Sea Pines Resort and Conference Center at Hilton Head Island, South Carolina. I went to Charlie to suggest we take the wives along, and he liked the idea, as did Dennis. I'm sure Charlie told his wife, Anne, it was his idea.

We rented a condo owned by a doctor, and it was replete in every way—amazing for a time-share. We looked forward to dining out at some fine restaurants and to playing a round of golf at the very famous Harbour Town Links, where the Heritage Classic is played every year. It is a favorite venue for many of the best golfers in the PGA. We had the same pecking order to name our choice of restaurant, and Dennis and I hosted at the best-rated ones we could find in the immediate area, to our complete satisfaction.

The third day Charlie stunned us with this announcement: "Ah went to the supermarket and picked up a beef roast. Anne is preparing a nice home-cooked dinner for us." Oh, there he goes again! Dennis and I exchanged that knowing look we were getting practiced at.

The highlight of the week for Dennis and me was the prospect of playing golf at Harbour Town on Friday. My enthusiasm was quieted somewhat because I hurt my leg the first afternoon when I dove into the Atlantic and thought something, perhaps a jellyfish, had stung me in the left leg. It turned out to be a muscle tear or a broken blood vessel, and I couldn't get my left heel down to the ground, vital for a right-handed golfer. Still, I was determined to play. It took weeks for my leg to heal.

Meet the Nuns

My father-in-law, George, was of English heritage and had four
brothers, Ralph, Gord, Allie, and Herbert (Hub); a stepbrother,
Ken; and one sister, Elaine, who lived in Chicago. I met her just
one time. I knew Ralph and Gord quite well, as Ralph was the
coach and Gord the sponsor of the basketball team I played for
in the Industrial League. They were both personable guys, with
Gord being especially outgoing while running his tavern business.
Hub was a cop, and he was the policeman who shot my dog when
Brownie was hit by a train, the Northwestern 400.

If George had a relationship with any of his bothers, it was
with Allie on occasion. Ralph and George lived within sight of
each other's houses, but that was the only closeness I observed.
This was very much unlike my family, where both sides were close.
The Ernsts and the Thomacks had annual reunions, usually at a
ballroom with an orchestra playing polka, waltz, and schottische
numbers. My father rarely missed a dance.

Bernice, my mother-in-law, was French and had four brothers and eight sisters. Three of her sisters entered the convent as
very young women. They were Rose (who died at an early age),
Germaine, and Colombiere. Sister Germaine was stoic and stern
but had one redeeming side to her, as she loved and knew professional baseball very well. She once coached a boys' team in
Chicago and won a state championship with them. I never met
any of the brothers.

Colombiere was just the opposite, as she was very attractive,
even in her habit, and so easygoing and fun-loving. She made you
feel like you were old friends. Germaine may have already been
retired when I first met her, but Colombiere was still semi-active
in Florida, where she taught French to Jewish people, which I
thought was rather peculiar.

I had no idea what the nuns' daily routine might have been except for one thing: happy hour. They took a break every afternoon at four o'clock to toast the good life with Manhattan cocktails.

During one of their annual vacation stays with the in-laws, the nuns came to Sheboygan to spend some time with my wife and me. I was prepared for their visit and broke out the Manhattans at the appointed hour, to their surprise and delight. A moment of hilarity came as our friend, Kenny, happened to stop by while we were having our drinks. He took one look at Colombiere and blurted out, "Boy, I'd like to hustle you."

Colombiere took to him instantly too, bursting into almost uncontrollable laughter while hugging the daylights out of him. Germaine disapproved; she just stiffened some more and remained her stoic self, incapable of letting her hair down and enjoying a moment of levity.

Bernice flew to Detroit, where the nuns were residing in a retirement community and celebrating their Diamond Jubilee—sixty years of dedication. Meanwhile, George didn't accompany Bernice and stayed back in Neenah. He would fly only if he could keep one foot on the ground. He died suddenly from a massive heart attack during her absence.

Roger and Ken

Roger Dugan, the sales and engineering director, appeared to be a fine gentleman in all respects and was well liked by his employees, including his good friend Hans Deiter. Roger had a sweet, lovely wife, Sophia, who was very attentive to him. My wife and I associated with them and at times were hosted on his sixty-foot Hatteras yacht along with the Deiters. It was rumored that Roger was enamored with Hans's wife, Risa. She was somewhat attractive but had a mouthful of really large teeth and was called Horse Face behind her back by those who weren't endeared to her.

One night after bowling, I decided to stop for a sandwich before heading for home. I bumped into Roger, who'd had the same thought. When we didn't find a place open, he said, "Robbie, let's go to my office for a nightcap. I've got a bottle of brandy in my credenza."

We talked about everything, and one drink led to another. It was about three in the morning when he decided to ring up Risa. She answered the phone immediately, and Roger started, "Hello, dahlink," and kept on sweet-talking her, confirming the rumors.

Another time, I dropped my dog off at the vet's office before going to work and spotted Roger and Risa sitting together in a car parked on a side street. Horse Face and all, Risa had something that appealed to Roger. We've heard it before: Looks aren't everything.

One Saturday morning, after our usual round of golf, Reuben, Bony (who was another good neighbor), and I opted to go into town for a few beers at the popular Wiess's Tavern, where prices were cheaper than at the golf course's bar. Rudy, the owner, always called me "Junior," probably because he didn't know my name.

A guy acquainted with Reuben and Bony walked over to us, and we were introduced. He was unshaven and seemed a little seedy, but was well-spoken and inquisitive, wanting to know what I did for a living. Ken was unemployed and looking for a job. Subsequently, he contacted me a number of times until he convinced me to give him a listen. It was evident he was well-versed in manufacturing processes, had experience, and could recite NPT numbers.

I agreed to try to get him an interview with Roger, who didn't agree until I asked him a second time. Roger hired Ken as a project engineer, and I saw him in a completely different light versus the first impression.

Ken must have wanted to show his appreciation to me, because he would stop at my office door after work every day and ask me to go have one with him. I always declined and said I didn't do that. Previously, he called me at my bowling team sponsor's place, knowing the team always went there after bowling. He insisted I come to meet him at Billy's Scenic Bar, popular for food[1] and drinks and owned by his uncle, who favored "canaries," as he called the shots he drank. Again, I declined, but Ken was adamant that I come because he was with his wife, Joanne, and he wanted to introduce us. So I went.

When I got there, they had a steak sandwich ready for me. In time, Ken and I became really good friends, as did our wives, and we became a regular foursome.

Ken and I got to know each other much better one winter morning when we were the only two to show up for work because we were having such a severe blizzard no one else made it in. Well, blizzards be damned, the bars are always open, so we took off, and he took me to Melody Bar.

Trinity Downtown

Finding a church I wanted to attend was always a priority for me when moving into a new community, and I found my church after visiting a number of them in the city. Trinity Lutheran, standing across from the public library and often referred to as Trinity Downtown to differentiate it from other churches of the same name in the area, was over a hundred years old, and its

---

[1] Subscribers to the Milwaukee *Journal Sentinel* could write the food editor to ask her to obtain the recipe for a given dish enjoyed at a given establishment. The chefs acquiesced at times and sometimes declined to do so. A request was made for Greena Bona, a German-Russian soup the Scenic Bar served and I always favored. Billy provided the recipe but it made twelve gallons

interior décor was reminiscent of the Old World churches I saw in Germany, which I loved for the ambiance. Trinity was the mother church of numerous other churches, and daughter congregations included Bethlehem, St. Paul, Immanuel, and Redeemer.

Shortly after I joined the church, I was asked to sit on the church council. When a certain issue was being discussed, I said "Should that happen ..." and was challenged by a longstanding member of the congregation. He said, "What do you mean, it *should* happen?"

I explained I meant *if* that were to happen, not that it *should* happen. Sometimes we speak the same but different languages.

I soon learned plans were set for a $1.5 million renovation—big money in 1968. Renovation included a complete redesign of the church entrance with dual enclosed stairways, whereas the original had exposed steps. Each stairway had steps to an upper landing that was receiving new stained glass treatment. A second flight of stairs reached the vestibule and nave. An elevator ran between the floors but not up to the balcony.

The east and west transcepts also had balconies, but they were removed to comply with some ordinance of the fire department. The white painted altar and woodwork was replaced with stained furnishings. The apse was completely redesigned with a large rose window above the altar.

This renovation was the first of a series of future major projects, undertaken whether by choice or necessity. Remodeling the school, adding a gymnasium, and making over the library required expenditures of $350,000 to $450,000. Then the church bought a medical clinic just a block away for one million bucks, plus more for modifications, and that was followed by another million dollars to rebuild the organ, which took about eight months. Next came roof replacement, costing another $470,000.

Currently, there was a fund drive to raise $260,000 for a new boiler. The old clinic became the Ministry Center and provided space for the 3K program, which had reached maximum enrollment level. As for me, I didn't think it was a good decision at the time. Trinity had truly been blessed with a faithful membership with sufficient wealth to support such extraordinary expenses. It had also been blessed with dedicated pastors, teachers, and gifted music directors. Music is an important part of our worship and explains why we are sometimes called the Singing Church.

Trinity had two parsonages. The larger and older was just a block away from the church, while the second was a cozy lannon stone place situated on a dead-end street on the east side of town. I don't know for certain when and why the parsonage program was discontinued, but I believe the current head pastor at the time, Rev. Harvey Krueger, may not have been satisfied with the old parsonage and preferred to have a private residence. The pastor and associate pastor were given housing allowances, and the parsonages were sold.

Rev. and Mrs. Krueger built a rather spacious ranch home across the street from my future friend, Kenny. Pastor Krueger smoked L&M cigarettes, and Kenny, ever showing his comedic side, said L&M stood for Lutheran Minister. Pastor was known to smoke one of Kenny's Marlboro cigarettes when he was out. Kenny teased him about having canned sermons with numbers assigned to them for reference.

Kenny himself attended grade school at Trinity and remembered his lessons well, so he was comfortable with Pastor Krueger for a neighbor. Apparently, Kenny joined Joanne's church, St. John's UCC, after marriage, but they didn't attend services.

Pastor Krueger was kind of a shouter in the pulpit. I prefer to have my pastor speak in a more confidential manner, and that's exactly what we found in Pastor Schmidt, who accepted the call after Krueger retired. My wife, who hadn't yet converted, said she wanted Pastor Schmidt at her deathbed. Mrs. Schmidt, Mabel, was both music and choir director. The annual Christmas candlelight service became so popular under her direction it was necessary to schedule a second performance. If you wanted a seat, you had better arrive at least half an hour early.

Along Came Phil

The Thomas Industries president, Thomas Fuller, announced the company was going to build a new facility for the Sheboygan operations. Fuller persuaded an old business associate, Philip Morrison, to come out of retirement to oversee the construction. Morrison was pompous and flatulent, letting all know he was condescending to come to Sheboygan, even though it was just for a temporary assignment. First impressions aren't always fair or accurate, but there was little reason for change as things progressed.

The first order of business was to negotiate the purchase of land for the plant site. The question was how much to purchase, and Phil and I disagreed about that. I felt we should buy the entire piece of acreage to allow for possible future expansion. The excess, if not needed, could be sold. Also, the land might not be available in the future and for certain would come at a greater cost. Phil thought the possibility of future growth was too remote. He was long gone when the company paid a premium to get the extra property.

Tom Fuller called Phil almost every day to talk about the progress being made, and he usually called right after lunch hour. Phil was seldom available. Since our offices were adjacent to each other, I could often hear Phil explaining he was at the construction site checking this or that. Cell phones weren't in existence yet, so land phones were the only means of direct communication, and that helped Phil cover his tracks.

I knew where he was, and it usually wasn't at the plant site. He was at the Executive Inn drinking his lunch and shaking dice with his cronies, including the owner of the hotel. I was tempted to take one of Fuller's calls to tell him where Phil could be reached, but I never did. Perhaps I should have.

Construction was moving right along, with or without Phil's presence, and I worked up a spreadsheet to help track it. I listed all the contractors, subcontractors, projects, and vendors with the contract costs. Posting the billings as received gave a current picture of the progress and pointed out what needed priority attention. I think it proved to be a very helpful aide to meeting target dates for completion.

Meanwhile, Kenny was working on his third engineering project at the old plant. It was larger than the previous ones. A proposed project had to have a satisfactory payback period to get expenditure authorization. Charlie wasn't always cooperative, even though the projects were designed to improve quality and efficiency.

It was believed that man-hours were part of Charlie's performance evaluation, and protecting them was the reason he was reluctant to support Kenny's projects. I don't know what equipment Kenny's latest project was bringing in, but it was finally delivered, and the huge crate just sat and sat and sat in the receiving department. Charlie wasn't going to move it into the plant.

Kenny and I were having lunch when, fortified by a martini, he told me he was going in to see Phil to explain the problem he was having with Charlie and hoped to get his support. I told him I'd tackle him if I saw him heading for Phil's office. I could see out into the general office area from my office, so I'd see him coming. Phil had the corner office, and mine was adjacent to it.

I didn't see it happen, but somehow Kenny slipped into Phil's office. Moments later, he came into mine to say, "Well, I'm done. Phil said that under the circumstances, the best solution was for me to leave."

Phil had been out to lunch too, and he wasn't going to

confront Charlie, who resented his being there in the first place. Manufacturing efficiency and bottom line weren't of any concern to him. I wondered whether I should have tried to reason with Phil. Ultimately, Kenny's departure may have been the best thing for him, as he got a job in the engineering department at Haysson, manufacturer of flexible packaging equipment and inventor of the first automatic bread-wrapping machine, and he didn't have to deal with the likes of Charlie and Phil.

Now it was my turn to make a decision. Phil came into my office and told me Louisville wanted me to be the corporate chief accountant. Charlie had told me over and over that corporate was a place to avoid, as it was an executive graveyard. The company's practice was to hire an outside consulting firm on a short-term basis until it determined which consultant it wanted to hire away. It was much cheaper to operate that way than to pay full fees to the firm. Once the consultant completed a specific assignment, he'd be fired, as his services were no longer required.

I declined the job offer, and Phil came back with a counter-offer that I also declined without hesitation. After the fourth and "final" offer, I told Phil I'd discuss it further with my wife. Except for dealing with Charlie and Phil, I was content where I was and not looking for a change. We had a nice home, great friends, liked the community, and were near our families. I liked my work, and my wife was very happy in her job as a sales associate at J. C. Penney Co.

The only problem I foresaw was this: I'd always heard that employees who passed up promotions were blackballed and wouldn't get further consideration for advancement, plus future compensation might be impacted. Charlie's warnings about Louisville being an executive graveyard didn't really concern me, because I didn't think the corporate chief accountant position would be subject to that possibility, so I accepted the offer. Had we not enjoyed living in Louisville so much, I doubt I'd have made the change regardless of what refusing it might entail.

Note: The Thomas Industries business in Sheboygan was purchased by Gardner-Denver, which subsequently moved the operation to Monroe, Louisiania, following an unresolved labor dispute.

My favorite sign found in a Sheboygan pub: "If you drive your husband to drink, drive him here."

CHAPTER 12

Sheboygan in the Rearview Mirror

Janet and I were excited and looking forward to finding a new home in Louisville as we flew into Standiford Field. We stayed at the Brown Hotel, famous for its Hot Brown sandwich[2]* and located just a couple of blocks away from the Thomas Industries headquarters on Broadway. Having only three days for house-hunting puts a lot of pressure on you, as you'll be making a big decision.

There was nothing available in our old neighborhood. We narrowed our choices down to three houses and ultimately decided two of them were too grand for us. One was a brand-new place and would require getting window treatments for the entire house, which could be quite expensive in itself. A coworker once told me it takes three years to recover from a transfer, and here we'd be taking on a bigger mortgage along with a higher interest rate.

The house we agreed on was thirteen miles from downtown Louisville, so I'd have a daily commute—which I liked, because I

---

[2] A Sheboygan restaurant served a version of the Hot Brown and called it a Whitehorse sandwich. It was slices of turkey breast over toast points with a mushroom sauce covered with cheese and bacon. It was finished off under the broiler. Just delicious.

could do some preplanning as I drove in. Actually, it was a pretty fast drive, except when traffic backed up as gawkers had to slow to see why a vehicle was off the road. The house was a five-bedroom two-and-a-half-bath New Orleans colonial with a wrought-iron façade on the second floor and built on a rise so the back of the house was three stories high. The lower level served as underground parking and also had a large, sunny laundry room.

We hoped to assume the owner's mortgage as we had the other time we bought in Kentucky so we could better the going rates for new loans. But the balance was too low, requiring a much higher down payment. Our house sold quickly to a Chinese couple, and Janet set up a moving sale on a Saturday morning. When I came home from golfing, I found she had sold all my bar equipment, glasses, stools, refrigerator, and my treasured Budweiser lamps I had mounted on the back bar. I had loaned them to Reuben to use in his basement bar with the proviso that I wanted them back if I ever finished my basement, which I did with a divided bar and lounge area. Kenny, Joanne, Janet, and I were Pabst Blue Ribbon fans, but still, the Budweiser lamps were a nice finishing touch. As per usual, I never saw any of the moving sale proceeds.

We were about to depart for Louisville when Kenny stopped by to say goodbye. His eyes were pretty watery, and that caused my tear ducts to overflow too. It was really hard to leave the good friend he'd become. You can have a lot of acquaintances, but really good friends are hard to find. It always troubled me when I saw friends go their separate ways after a falling out over some silly thing. I always told myself I'd never let pride hurt a friendship I valued, and I never did.

It was only a couple of weeks earlier that Kenny had told me his bachelor brother was buying a new car and wanted to sell the old car outright. It had very low mileage, so I bought it, as my Buick Electra mileage was getting up there and I was considering buying a new car anyway. We drove off in the emerald-green Chrysler.

On Broadway

Upon reaching Louisville, we checked the location of Thomas Industries' corporate offices and found it was on Broadway in downtown Louisville. We booked a room at the Holiday Inn until our household furnishings arrived two days later. I don't know why it took that long, but the delay gave us a chance to relax for a couple of days, even though I reported for work the next day.

For a change, I wasn't walking into a vacancy. The current chief accountant, Milton Reeves, wasn't leaving for another week, so I had a chance to understand the basics of the job before he left. Milton was highly intelligent and threw around words like *eclectic, éclat, esoteric,* etc.—a nearly foreign language to me at times. His reason for leaving was that he wanted to go back to his roots in Oregon.

Within two days, one wouldn't know we had just moved into the house. Janet had very good organizational skills and experience in settling a place, as this was our seventh move. I always made myself scarce, having to go to the office, as I hated the disorganization. She probably liked me being out of her way.

The emerald green Chrysler wasn't equipped with air-conditioning, plus it had a large transmission housing located on the floor between the driver and passenger sides that emitted a ton of heat, so I tacked a for-sale sign on the bulletin board of the supermarket where we did our grocery shopping. To my surprise, I received a call the next day and sold the car for my asking price. I had driven Buicks for years with complete satisfaction, so I bought another one, a LeSabre. I was walking to the office from the parking lot when our president, Tom Fuller, joined up with me. He said, "I drive a Chevrolet." Strike one.

Several months later, I was at the annual stockholders' meeting, and there was still a half hour before the start of the business meeting, so I ordered a second cocktail. Mr. Fuller walked up to me and said, "I had only one." Strike two.

The NCAA basketball tournament was coming up, and Louisville had a good team and a Hall of Fame coach in Denny Crum, so there was lot of local interest in the tournament. Denny won 675 of 970 games, a .696 percentage. He reached the Final Four six times and won national champion twice. Tom Fuller attended every home game.

The office pool was run by Kevin Draeger from the audit department, and he was a rah-rah Notre Dame grad. The entry fee was five dollars, and you could enter as often as you wanted. With all the local interest, I figured the pool might have upwards of $500 in it. I picked Michigan State, the eventual winner. One other person picked MS, too, and Kevin gave us our winnings: $27.50, as he claimed there was only $55 in the pool.

I questioned that in my mind but didn't pursue the matter. Obviously, there was something amiss. Kevin had nervous, darting eyes, just like a salesman back at the Sheboygan operation. I'd meet two more like him later.

Imagine my surprise when Tom Fuller took me along on a trip to the West Coast. Our first visit was to the Portland facility, which made top-of-the-line fireplace equipment and tools, and the visit was non-eventful. From there we flew to Los Angeles to check out the foundry. We had dinner with the plant manager, Mark Jensen, and I made sure to choose a moderately priced entrée. After dinner, Fuller said, "Let's go to the lounge, Mark. I want to talk to you." Mark drove a Cadillac, so he had a strike against him, too.

I tried to excuse myself, but Fuller insisted I stay with them. We ordered a second drink—wow!—and then the ripping started. It was embarrassing to witness it, and I was sure Mark was going to be fired on the spot. But he survived.

Fuller walked out ahead of us. I shook Mark's hand with a knowing handshake and patted him on the back.

Next, I was sent to Little Rock with the company engineer and no directions. I guessed it was just for me to become familiar with another of our thirteen locations. Little Rock was a glass plant where elements were made for the residential lighting division. Some pieces were molded, while glass blowers made what items weren't in mass production. Little Rock used two types of molds, and I spent two days analyzing the maintenance history. One kind had a much higher repair record, and the total difference was quite material. I should have inquired if there was a reason for using a certain mold. Also, I should have reviewed my findings with the engineer, but I told myself there was a reason for the two types of molds and eventually junked the report.

I didn't get to all the locations but did go to Cleveland; Cincinnati; Johnson City, Tennessee; Fort Atkinson; Grand Rapids; the Chicago lighting center; and Shakopee, Minnesota. I thought I was being groomed for something.

Fuller was always pushing for month-end results and would come to my office to ask about a specific location. On one occasion, I said the controller hadn't reported in yet, and he said, "How come? I've got it." Then he'd ask if I knew anything about a certain plant manager, because he said, as he thrust his middle fingers skyward, "I'd like to stick it to him." Another suspicious mind?

Visitors

Kenny and Joanne visited us several times. Kenny couldn't wait to check out the construction of our house, expecting it to be substandard. He ran his fingers over the painted woodwork like a blind person reading Braille. He found quality workmanship and was impressed with the pocket doors between the kitchen dinette area and the dining room, and the family room, which had a pegged wooden floor reminiscent of those found on expensive yachts. During the first visit, we went to see *The Stephen Foster Story* in Bardstown. It was a fantastic performance, and the songs included "My Old Kentucky Home," "Swanee River," and "Beautiful Dreamer."

The next day, we went to an Amish community where they made straw brooms by hand. It was a very interesting insight into the Amish lifestyle. On their next visit, we had another unforgettable experience when we spent a weekend in Nashville.

The next time we saw them was for our daughter's wedding back in Wisconsin, and this time we were their guests. Our daughter wanted a certain band, Buffalo Joe, at the church, and they played "On Eagle's Wings," and the soloist gave a wonderful rendition. The reception was at the Town and Country Golf Club, and we had 180 guests, the maximum number allowed. We had a pretty good orchestra, a champagne fountain, and an open bar that I intended to cut off at eight o'clock but decided to let run all evening.

I returned to work on the following Monday, and at four o'clock I was told that my boss, Ed Chady, wanted me in his office. Ed said, "Have a seat, Bob, I have something to tell you. Our business backlog has dropped off the table, and we are releasing seven department heads. I'm sorry to tell you that you're one of them."

Naturally, I was stunned, but I gathered myself and asked how they were going to get through the month-end reporting coming up. Ed just shrugged his shoulders. I asked if anyone else knew I was being fired, and he said, "No." I offered to stay on through the reporting period, and he agreed to it.

The next morning, I was standing at the top of the stairway on the second floor as people were coming up. Don Black, the head auditor, looked up and saw me. If a head could fly off from a double take, his would have been in orbit. Yes, Ed, no one else knew. Black had been hired away from Ernst & Young, eventually becoming company president, an exception to the executive graveyard business.

Déjà Vu

Janet was just as stunned as I had been when I broke the news to her. She was enjoying working with the other sales associates at Penney's and had developed a following of customers seeking her out for her help, as she had a flair for dressing them in the women's and petite department, just as she had back in Wisconsin. Leaving Kentucky again would be very difficult for us, as we couldn't have been happier with our home, neighbors, climate, and lifestyle. I'd also miss the semitropical plants, flowering bushes, shrubs, and trees, especially my favorite magnolias.

Eventually, we did decide to return to Wisconsin, simply because three of our children and almost all of our relatives were there. We still had our twelve-year-old son, John, with us. There were potential opportunities in Louisville, as GE had a huge plant there with such a vast parking lot that traffic was controlled by regular stop and go signals. Ford had a similar-sized operation within a mile of our place. I was confident my résumé would draw response from at least one of them, but I didn't pursue either, as we had made the decision to return to Wisconsin.

I wasn't very hopeful of finding work there with the recession we were in, but I responded to an ad in the *Sheboygan Press* for an assistant controller—better than nothing under the circumstances. I did get a response to my inquiry with an interview and follow-up call to come in for a test. Unlike the Thomas test, which was heavily mathematics, this one was a psychological examination at Manitowoc, the headquarters and ice cream plant for Lake to Lake Dairy Cooperative.

I got hired, and the starting salary was exactly what I had been making at Thomas. The job duties were also identical to those I'd had as a controller previously, including budget preparation and pro forma statements to start.

Now it was back to Kentucky to take care of business there. I found a snowball in the freezer … in July? It was a hailstone the size of a baseball, and Janet had saved it because she didn't think I'd believe it otherwise. Our roof had to be replaced before we could put the house on the market, and we had to find Janet a new car, as hers was all dinged up from the storm.

A rather young couple came through the house the second day it was listed in a publication put out by the local real estate association with all the agencies' listing by area. The woman was crazy for the house, but the husband seemed doubtful to me. Still, the next day, we received an acceptable offer, and our moving plans were set, as we had already purchased a nice ranch home in Sheboygan.

It was moving day, and the movers were about to wrap things up when the buyer's agent appeared. We expected to see him at the closing, not at the house. He was a little old balding guy, probably in his sixties. He stammered something I didn't understand, cleared his throat, coughed, and caught his upper plate as it flew out of his mouth. Finally, he got the words out: "I'm afraid I have some bad news for you. The buyers are backing out of the deal."

Apparently, the husband thought the house was beyond their means. Now the house had been off the market for a month due to the accepted offer status, or we likely would have had some other interested parties. The final blow was that we had to return the earnest down payment money, another difference in Kentucky law vs. Wisconsin. Why require earnest money in the first place if it is meaningless?

Now we had to make another decision: unpack and stay, or proceed with the move? It's common knowledge an empty house doesn't sell as well as a furnished one, because it just doesn't show as well. Nevertheless, we were confident such a beautiful place would sell even with the recession casting a pall over the general real estate market, and we let the movers finish packing.

It was bad enough having a mortgage on the new place at 16 percent interest, but now we had two mortgages to contend with, and it would take almost six months for our place on Boxford Way to sell.

CHAPTER 13

Lake to Lake Dairy Cooperative

L
ake to Lake came onto the Sheboygan scene when it merged with Modern Dairy, whose beginning dated back to 1902 when milk was delivered by horse-drawn wagons. Lake to Lake itself was formed in 1945 when a group of farmers organized in an effort to combat depressed milk prices. They recruited Truman Torgerson, the Manitowoc county agent, as general manager, and the co-op expanded across the eight counties in Northeast Wisconsin that had the densest milk cow population in the Dairy State, and membership increased to over two thousand producers.

In addition to the Sheboygan plant, which bottled milk and made cultured products, cottage cheese, and sour cream, Lake to Lake had three other plants: Denmark made butter and Italian cheeses; Manitowoc made premium ice creams; and Kiel made cheddar cheese and was the largest operation. Roland Tess was the head cheesemaker, and his cheeses won many blue ribbons in statewide contests and won the World Cheese Championship.

I looked forward to going to the plant just for the fresh cheese curds, which were still warm, salty, and squeaky to eat. Land O' Lakes was the biggest customer, as it bought forty-pound blocks as they came off the machines. Private labeling generated another sizeable portion of the overall sales.

One problem with cheesemaking is that for every pound of cheese made, you wind up with nine pounds of whey, and disposing of it creates a problem. It was common practice to spread whey on farmlands, but that can be harmful to the environment. Lake to Lake's answer was to build a huge whey-drying facility, and dried whey became a profit maker rather than an expense. Dried whey is a valuable ingredient in food and confectionary products for its high nutritional value. It can be found in candies, bakery products, snack foods, yogurts, dips, desserts, meat and pasta products, ice cream, soups, sauces, beverages, processed cheese, sport drinks, and health foods.

My new superior was William Hartziem, and it didn't take long to discover he was different, weird. My office had a large window, so I could see his office and up the hallway to the general accounting area and the men's room. We shared a secretary, Mary Buzaitis, and she was by far the best secretary I ever had. No one could type faster, and she made that IBM Selectric typewriter—the model with the ball instead of arms for the individual letters—really hum. It was fascinating and amazing to watch the ball fly around.

Mary would have a report done almost as fast as I could get back to my office. She had a very good grasp of grammar, but she also had the bluest vocabulary of anyone I knew, as I found out when she came into my office to vent her frustration with Willy.

Mary wasn't allowed to open Willy's mail except to slit the envelopes. Willy would open an envelope, remove the contents, close the envelope for a couple of seconds, then rip it open, peer into it, close it again for a few seconds, rip it open—and he'd do this three or four times with each envelope. He did a similar thing when he went to the men's room: whip the door open, peer into the restroom, stand back, close the door, whip it open, peer in, and close the door again before finally entering the room. He'd do the same thing when he exited the room. He'd close the door, wait a couple of seconds, whip the door open, and peer inside. Again, he repeated this three or four times. This kind of behavior would manifest itself later at a critical time.

Willy, Willy

We were experiencing an abnormal number of questionable lost-time accidents, usually by the youngest employees, while the nature of our operations didn't involve any hazardous or risky tasks. Safety wasn't in my area of responsibility, but I looked into safety programs anyway, and I found Safety Bingo as being something worth trying. I suggested it to the plant manager. He liked the prospect of reducing lost-time incidents, and we got approval to initiate the program. A number was drawn for each accident-free day, and we offered cash prizes. If an accident were to occur, the number drawn for that day would be voided rather than a starting a new game, which would have set a negative tone and be unfair to the rest of the employees.

The first lost-time event happened in the sixth or seventh week, after a number of bingo winners. The lost time "accident" happened to be on my bowling day, and, as usual, we went to our sponsor's establishment for refreshments afterward. Some guys were playing pool, and who do I spot but the person who was out? When he noticed me, he merely put his pool cue back in the rack and disappeared. He was at work the next day.

We had two payroll clerks—one for our semi truck drivers and milk haulers, the other for the regular plant employees. I did an audit for the latter and discovered errors in applying contract provisions amounting to more than my salary. We couldn't recover the overpayments, but the savings would be realized year after year. We had to justify our existence during our annual review, and this was a measureable asset for me.

Willy and I had an appointment with Time Insurance in Milwaukee to negotiate the renewal rates for our producers' health insurance plan. Riding with Willy was a different experience. He'd get up to the speed limit and coast down to about forty miles per hour, speed back up, coast, speed up, coast ... all the way to Milwaukee.

When we arrived at Time Insurance, the security guard who checked us in said he was an amateur graphologist, and would we mind if he analyzed our signatures, to which we both agreed. Quite quickly he was finished, and in words to that effect, told Willy he was nuts. Willy was miffed and stalked off.

It didn't take Willy long to prove this guy was no amateur. Our meeting was with Warren Mielke, a vice president, and he readily got to the crux of our meeting, telling us of the rate increase for the coming contract period. Willy jumped up, ripped of his sport coat, put up his fists, and assumed a classic John L. Sullivan stance. He challenged Warren, who was shocked but kept his cool, and Willy backed off. There was little discussion after that, and the meeting ended with the ball in our court. Willy and I rode home in silence. I was angry and then had to endure the ride back. Speed up, coast, speed up ...

Our meeting with the board of directors was held the next day in Manitowoc. Of course, Willy's recommendation was to make the change to another insurer, and he didn't expand on his position. The board asked for my opinion.

I didn't think we had to make an immediate decision. First of all, and Willy didn't mention this, we had been told there would be no coming back if we left Time. The bridge would be burned. I thought we should try to renegotiate to seek a premium reduction by introducing a deductible and copayments, which were absent from the existing plan. The other insurer being considered was lowballing, a common practice in the industry to get a foot in the door. Finally, enrolling our 2,000 milk producers, spread over eight counties, in a new plan would be a formidable process.

Would the board go against Willy, my superior, or listen to the second fiddle? They sided with Willy. To this day, I regret not reporting Willy's John L. Sullivan antic, but at the time, I thought surely the board would give renegotiating a chance before making a final decision. Plus, I had to work with Willy, but the good of the business should have prevailed. Mea culpa!

Something that couldn't be considered at this time, but for future reference, was a self-insured program. I did a projection using our current premiums, and it appeared quite feasible to me. A third party (TPA) actually administers the plan. Catastrophic losses could be mitigated by stop-loss provisions or reinsurance from the likes of Lloyds of London. Little did I know that future consideration would never become a possibility.

Speak Up, Bob

Lake to Lake was organized with districts to facilitate addressing the membership, and I prepared the usual three-dimensional graphics to depict performance and comparisons. I used different colored cellophanes inlaid in the designs to give life to the overheads. For the upcoming meetings, I had an unusual topic to project, and it was just one of the eight overheads.

Truman Torgerson conducted the regular part of the meeting and then presented a proposal from Land O' Lakes to merge Lake to Lake into the Land O' Lakes complex formed by the acquisition of many related businesses. The last of the overheads was related to the merger proposal, and Truman turned off the projector without showing it.

I was anxious to see the members' response to it, but Truman pulled it, knowing it would certainly cause a negative reaction and scuttle the proposal. The missing overhead related to the annual administrative fee Land O" Lakes intended to charge Lake to Lake, and I'm sure there'd have been a collective gasp from the members, because it was $1 million. This is where I should have questioned why he was withholding the key element of the proposal. I think it was deceitful and a cover-up, as Truman knew it would defeat the proposal.

I wondered who else knew about this provision. Willy certainly should have, although he never mentioned it, and hadn't the board of directors been informed? In my mind, I didn't see any positive aspects to persuading the membership to accept the deal, even without the administrative fee issue, which surely would have ruined us. I had heard that Truman was getting $350,000 to promote the merger, and his conduct only reinforced that possibility. To me, there was no other explanation. Did the fact that Truman was retiring have any bearing on this?

I was excused from the balance of the district meetings. Was there concern I'd speak up? One option I considered was to contact someone on the board just to confirm its awareness of what was happening. Woulda, coulda … didn't. The motion carried at every district.

Hello and Goodbye

I never expected to meet another Philip Morrison, but Land O' Lakes sent Jerry Eckstein to replace the current manager. Jerry surpassed Phil in narcissism and self-aggrandizement. He also declared that none of us had any flamboyancy, but not to worry, as he had plenty for everybody. Jerry must have been an extremely heavy person at one time, judging by the way the seat of his trousers sagged down to the back of his knees. An elephant's ass would have fit in them with room to spare.

The first thing Jerry did was to convert our conference room into a grand office for himself. Some people wondered if he'd been sent to run our location into the ground, because he had managed a beer distributorship and seemed to know nothing about the dairy business. He changed the thrust of our sales efforts by catering to the Chicago market and shipping truckloads of product FOB Sheboygan. He and our transportation manager had a falling out because he was disrupting the regular flow of business by tying up so much of our fleet with Chicago deliveries, a 360-mile round trip.

When I realized what was happening to our bottom line, I developed a spreadsheet to analyze sales by measuring the gain or loss due to cost change, gain or loss due to volume change, and gain or loss due to price changes. Jerry never commented on it but did take some action. He reduced our plant sanitation practices. As a consequence, we wound up with a warehouse full of returned product which weren't keeping the indicated shelf life. Perhaps we were lucky not to have a salmonella outbreak.

On a Monday morning, the Land O' Lakes person now assigned to monitor our overall operation jumped all over me, demanding to know why I hadn't made an appearance on Sunday morning to assist in the sanitation work with all the other exempt salaried employees Jerry had ordered to report. I had not known about it. It was never mentioned to me, but he didn't believe that. Even if I had known, I might not have appeared, because my Sunday mornings are for church, and they couldn't deny that to me. Somehow the union employees didn't hear about this either, and Jerry got away with something here.

Jerry invited Janet and me to dinner at his house, and I forewarned her about the type of person Jerry was. Jerry's wife, Sylvia, was a charming, lovely lady, and I wondered what she saw in Jerry. At home, he showed a different personality altogether from his office demeanor. He was actually very gentlemanly and a considerate host.

My next run-in with the LOL guy who chewed me out over the sanitation business was over the budget for the coming year. He called me to find out what our bottom line was, and when I gave it to him, he said, "G-damn you. You get rid of that loss." What did he expect when we were absorbing a million-dollar administrative fee?

I left every budget item completely intact, except I adjusted the cost of milk procurement, our greatest expense, by the necessary figure.

Soon Jerry Eckstein was gone, and LOL replaced him with another manager, Clifford Miller, who called me to his office a couple of days after his arrival. He found my spreadsheet in Jerry's desk. At least he'd filed it, even if he ignored it otherwise. Clifford said, "I can see you were doing your job, and it's too bad Jerry didn't react to this information."

After a few months, we were notified that Land O' Lakes was shutting down the Sheboygan and Manitowoc operations. A local competitor, Verifine Dairy, attempted to buy the Sheboygan plant, but LOL refused the offer. That would have been a decent gesture for the existing clients. Instead, they sold it to Golden Guernsey in Waukesha. Golden Guernsey sold it to Dean Foods, and Dean Foods ultimately sold it to Verifine. The Manitowoc ice cream business was sold to Cedar Crest Dairy. Land O' Lakes got what it coveted through the merger: our cheesemaking operations, plus the whey processing gem. The final insult came when Land O' Lakes refused to acknowledge we had been employees. Nice guys, eh?

CHAPTER 14

The Equitable

Janet wanted a new house for no special reason; she just wanted a new house. We had everything we wanted in this place, and I had finished the basement, springboarding off the experience I gained when Kenny helped me previously. This basement was much larger, because we had a ranch-style home now, whereas the other house was a two story edifice. At any rate, I was proud of the finished product, as I did it all on my own except for the electrical wiring, about which I didn't know AC from DC. I didn't want to give it up, but we have to do what we have to do to keep our wives happy.

After considerable planning, we came up with what we thought was the ideal layout. The plan included every feature each of us wanted, and I was actually getting quite excited thinking about the end result. I drew up rough plans and took them to an architect to get blueprints and specifications drawn up. The special trusses were ordered and delivered to the Kindt Lumber Company site on the south side of town.

Our house was sold to an engineer from Iowa who was taking a job with the Kohler Company. We had hoped to stay in the house until our new place was ready for occupancy, but the Carlsons had a teenage daughter and needed to establish residency to get her enrolled in school, and that ended the possibility. Not wanting to pass up the sale of our house, we put most of our household belongings in storage and rented an apartment.

Kaboom! That was the sound of our plans being blown to bits, because I no longer had a job myself and wondered who might be interested in hiring me at my then age. Yet almost immediately after our plant closing was announced, I had what was tantamount to three job offers. All three were from insurance companies, including the Equitable Assurance Society of the United States (the Equitable), MetLife, and Prudential. MetLife's offer included a book of six hundred customers. I never responded to Prudential. I suppose any idiot would have latched on to the Met offer, but I decided to go with the Equitable, which had the Lake to Lake pension and retirement plans, so I was acquainted with Mack and Orville, Equitable representatives.

I didn't realize until later that Mack hadn't been fully upfront coming into the agency. While it was tied to the Equitable as the broker dealer for securities-based products, it operated as an independent agency, which meant there was no health insurance or retirement plan, but still reported to the Milwaukee agency. Other than personal expenses, I had no fixed financial commitment to the agency except to share a portion of any sales income generated.

Now, the first order of business for me was to get licensed by the Wisconsin Commissioner of Insurance for health and life insurance products. During the study period, I was dead weight to the agency, which had four other agents, of which one was Mack's son-in-law; two secretaries; and a clerk. Plus, I had no income without making any sales, which I couldn't attempt without a license. The next step after passing the state exam was to prepare for the securities licenses, which are under the governance of the state and federal authorities, and that was no small undertaking for me. Many candidates fail the tests even after prolonged preparation, but I did pass both exams.

Finally, I could sell variable life insurance and annuity products, which the Equitable invented. None of the other agents engaged in mutual fund sales, and they were important to my market approach, which was to pursue IRA and 401(k) rollovers. I used a mix of stock and bond funds, the mix depending on the need for current income while proposing a suitable plan consistent with the client's risk tolerance, which was tested for. I did not actively promote life insurance sales, as from experience I found policies were allowed to lapse before completing the surrender penalty charge provisions, which resulted in commission recoveries.

Maintaining the licenses was an ongoing process, as there were periodic tests to deal with. Medicare Advantage plans, while not securities-based, still require passage of annual tests. Also, the State of Wisconsin requires continuing education credits—twenty-four credit hours every two years—which I thought was rather pointless, because you could earn the credits through accredited courses for any life or annuity product without regard to the actual products you sold. I satisfied the requirement with twenty-four hours on disability income insurance, which I never sold or intended to, even though I found the in-depth study very interesting.

Mark and Brenda

Success and failure are part of the insurance and investment business, and rejections were hard to understand and troubled me. However, there was an unexpected benefit, not in the form of compensation but in friendships that developed over the course of time through the many contacts you encounter. I nearly matched up a pair of them.

Brenda Mills was the widow of a client who died too soon after retiring. I saw her periodically to review and update her account, and I found her to be friendly and spirited. Mark Forman had recently retired and had me handle his 401(k) rollover. He, too, was a person you just were drawn to and wanted to get to know better.

His Social Security number told me was originally from out of state, and that turned out to be Pennsylvania, where his only child, a daughter, lived. Mark's wife had passed several years earlier. He spoke of planning to retire in Arkansas, and I suggested he hold off on the idea for now and went on to ask if he would be interested in meeting a certain lady I could picture him with if she were willing. Mark liked the prospect of meeting Brenda as I described her to him, and I said I would see if she had any interest in meeting him.

She did, but on one condition: I had to pick her up at her home to come to our place for cocktails before going out for dinner at the Riverdale Country Club. Mark was to be at my house, and Janet was to entertain him until Brenda and I arrived. Brenda said she was so nervous she needed a cocktail to calm her down, so we had brandy old-fashioneds at the bar in her basement. One wasn't sufficient, as she was still very anxious about meeting a stranger, so we had a second before heading to my house.

Matchmaking doesn't always work, of course, but it sure did in this case. There was an immediate attraction, almost like two magnets, and they joshed back and forth as though they'd known each other for a long time. Janet and I were thoroughly amused. Well, we went to dinner, and there was more of the kidding stuff.

Mark took Brenda home and forgot to go home himself, as they spent the night together. Mark later confided in me that he wasn't able to perform thanks to the intoxicating beverages, but that was the only failure. These two people seemed to be made for each other.

Mark's plan to retire in Arkansas was more than just wishful thinking, as he had gone ahead with the purchase of a place in the Ozarks, Bull Shoals, and he'd be leaving in about six weeks. But he didn't want to go without Brenda, so he proposed marriage. Brenda was afraid to marry, because she would lose the free life-time health insurance she had through her husband's employer. She had Medicare and could enroll in a Medicare Supplement plan or a Medicare Advantage plan, but things were moving too fast. The arrangement they agreed upon was for Brenda to visit mark in Bull Shoals once he was settled, but Brenda said she wasn't going to move to Bull Shit, Arkansas.

The White River flows through Bull Shoals and is a destination for trout fishermen. The Army Corps of Engineers built a hydro-electric power plant there to control flooding and provide power to the area, creating a man-made lake, Bull Shoals Lake, with over a thousand miles of shoreline. It was a bass fisherman's dream. Many international bass-fishing tournaments are held there, and it yields enormously big bass, including the world-record catch.

Brenda telephoned me about two weeks after Mark left and asked if I'd heard from him. Mark had been calling her three and four times every day. I wouldn't know what happened until I took him up on his invitation to visit him myself.

Here was the answer to Brenda's dilemma about Mark: Bull Shoals was located in a dry county, but alcoholic beverages were available at the VFW Club, where Mark was spotted sitting alone at the bar looking lost and forlorn. Several women sitting at a nearby table and were watching him. One of the women motioned with her index finger for Mark to come to the table. She'd heard that Mark had just recently move to Bull Shoals and his household goods were sitting there just as they had arrived, still boxed up. Now, Mark didn't know anything more than I did about setting up housekeeping, and he just didn't know where to start.

The lady who motioned to him now offered her services, and

she not only got the household goods in order, she also moved herself in shortly thereafter. Her name was Toy.

I expected someone with the name *Toy* to be Asian, but she was not. Toy was welcoming and pleasant to me, but she wasn't going to give Mark and me a chance to be alone to talk. She was nice to me and certainly not attractive in any sense. In fact, she probably belonged to the ilk my mother-in-law would classify as "homelier than a busted ass." Toy was a very tiny person, and she had a steel rod in her left leg. Mark had to be attracted to more than her outward appearance.

Mark owned large pontoon boat, and we all spent an afternoon on it without getting a bite. The man-made lake we were on—I don't know if it was Bull Shoals Lake—had crystal clear water, and you could see the tops of trees all leafed out far below the surface. The lake abounded with pontoon boats, and they were the only type permitted. Some had showers and charcoal grills mounted on them.

We were at a shopping center when I decided to look for a housewarming gift and found a floral shop where I picked out a plant I was familiar with. I asked the clerk if it was a perennial. She said, "No, it's a hibiscus." Hello? Mark planted the hibiscus outside and wrote me to say how pleased they were with it and marveled at the profuse blossoms it produced.

Mark and Toy got married on the boat the following June. Mark got out of bed the night before Thanksgiving, and Toy found him sitting in the living room the next morning, dead of a massive heart attack.

Viktor

When my telephone rang, I expected to be hearing from a client, but it was Hilda, a vigorous nonagenarian I knew from church, where we usually sat together. Hilda was one of thirteen children but had no children of her own, and her husband had been deceased for years.

Hilda had been sergeant in the army, and the regimen was never lost. I visited her a number of times at her condo, and she once told me she planned to sell it and take an apartment to make it easier for her surviving relatives to settle her final affairs. I asked her to let me know when she decided to do it, because I was interested in buying it directly from her. It was a corner unit on the first floor of the twenty-four-unit condo structure, with a nice patio and spacious yard.

Each condo unit had two large bedrooms, two full baths, a large living room, a dining area and a kitchen in an open concept. There was an island in the kitchen, and there were built-in features like a stacked washer-dryer unit.

Hilda asked me if I had heard about Viktor's accident, which had happened almost a week earlier. I had not, and I'd wondered why Viktor hadn't been around, as he usually came to my office a couple of times each week when I hadn't been to see him at his place. When he did come in, we'd talk at length unless I had an appointment.

Hilda told me that Viktor had fallen at home, and I could tell she was distraught over it. She said that he was at Luther Manor Health Care Center in Wauwatosa on the western edge of Milwaukee. The next day, I took a friend, Missy, along with me to visit Viktor. She had met him several times, and they'd just hit it off.

I didn't know if Hilda was aware of Viktor's condition, but I was not prepared for anything very serious, as Viktor was the strongest physical specimen I had ever met. He was just over six feet tall, robust, and powerful as the proverbial ox, with a bull neck. He also shaved his head.

Shocked and staggered, I couldn't believe Viktor's condition had resulted from a simple fall. He was unconscious, his mouth wide open, his tongue dried and split down the middle, with an undissolved pill resting on it. Viktor had become a great friend, and I couldn't control my emotions in front of Missy, as it was so crushing to see this man-mountain lying there helpless and obviously in a terminal state. He died two days later on October 4, his eightieth birthday.

My initial contact with Viktor had happened years earlier, when my wife and I were house-hunting. We looked at a property Viktor had listed, but it was too old and not to our liking. After that, I only saw him and his wife, Marie, in church, where they both sang in the choir—until we were named to the board of directors for the Lutheran Cemetery Association, on which I was the treasurer for a three-year term that kept getting extended; ultimately, I served for twenty-five years. The board met monthly, and Viktor usually hosted during his terms.

Viktor was a mason by trade and had a construction business. He made his fortune by converting places like old firehouses, schools, and office buildings into apartments or condos, often selling them for substantial profits, as the cost of acquisition to him was very minimal. His pride and joy was the twenty-four-unit condo structure he built from the ground up. He and Marie lived on the second floor in a unique layout.

All first-floor units had patios, while all the others had a balcony. The heat source was electrical panels built into the walls, and they provided uniform heat but were not efficient cost-wise. Viktor and Marie's unit had a sunken living room that was four or five steps down from the foyer, and that's where Viktor fell backward as he was ascending the steps.

Viktor was an enigma to me. He led a very simple lifestyle while being able to afford all the luxuries of life, but he just didn't indulge himself, even when I urged him to enjoy his wealth and be generous with himself. He and Marie had traveled to Africa and Italy, but traveling alone just has no appeal to most people. He was content with simple things and was happiest eating bratwurst, onions, beans, and potatoes. He was from a German-Russian family and accustomed to common foods. To German-Russians, fleisbrok and grotbrok were delicacies. *Fleishbrok* was a pastry filled with ground beef, cabbage, and onions, while *grotbrok* was similar but without the meat. I've had them, and they are a treat.

One didn't want to underestimate Viktor for all his seemingly simple ways, as he could be quite complex and complicated, with an eye for opportunities others overlooked. He could envision making a silk purse out of sow's ear, converting properties unwanted by others into purposeful, valuable assets. How else could a mason accumulate millions of dollars?

Here's an example: The city was abandoning a parking ramp abutting Viktor's condos. He bought it for exactly one dollar and offered it to our church across the street. The church elders declined to accept it, as it might present an expense to maintain. Furthermore, the municipal library stood across opposite of the church, and its parking lot was always open on Sundays to supplement the church's parking lot to its rear. In addition, there was on-street parking.

Viktor's way of dealing with the now seemingly worthless property was to build ten two-bedroom apartments on the upper level. The lower level was made available to the condo owners for underground parking, with access from the street or the alley that ran behind the condos. He built a social room to accommodate up to eighty people with a state-of-the-art kitchen and a restroom. This provided an opportunity for the residents to get to know their neighbors better, and they held regular potluck suppers that enhanced the bonding. Viktor turned the balance of the space into a recreation room with a pool table, a tool room that could supply a hardware store, and a storage room now filled with artwork he was holding as collateral for a huge loan he made to a local businessman.

I had been having a slow month at the office and decided to call Viktor to see if I could be of service to him. Marie answered the phone, and when I explained the purpose of my call, she asked without hesitation if $100,000 would help. There would be further positioning of the Wieners' liquid assets, even though they had been dealing with another representative for years.

Marie's father was the elder who challenged my use of *should* when he thought I meant it *ought to happen*, while I was merely saying *in the event that happens*. Marie had childhood-onset diabetes and died at the age of sixty-two, just a year after Viktor's sister, Freida. Just how sweet, well-liked, and friendly Marie was to everyone was evidenced by the overflow crowd that attended her funeral. Viktor gave $10,000 to the church to buy a new grand piano as a memorial to Marie, but it ended up costing him $17,000.

Viktor and Marie built a place on Legend Lake, a man-made 1,300-acre body of water with an irregular shoreline following the natural terrain, as there was no earth-moving done to disturb it. The lake was seventy feet at the deepest part, and there were long, narrow inlets, peninsulas, coves, and bays, but Viktor always knew exactly where he was when we went out on his pontoon boat. The lake was said to be populated with bass and trout, but we were unable to attest to that.

I called their place a lodge, but it was certainly more that. It had four bedrooms on the first floor on opposite sides of the great open area that made up the kitchen, dining room, and living room space with a large fireplace. There was a bathroom on each side between the bedrooms. The lower level had bedrooms, bath, shower, pool room, and storage area for the pontoon boat during the winter.

Legend Lake is on the Menominee Indian Reservation, and early builders often found their homes burned to the ground, as the white man was not welcome. However, that changed with time and the realization that the newcomers were good for the economy. There is an Indian casino nearby where people go for food and entertainment.

The neighbor to Viktor's left was his brother-in-law, Marie's brother, and his neighbor to the right was a retired fire chief from Chicago, a friendly fellow with a very gracious wife. They invited us over for cocktails.

I never heard Viktor utter anything close to a cuss word. He was a very generous man in many ways, especially if he liked you and trusted you.

He gave certain people use of the lodge whenever he wasn't going to be there himself, and the very same people were likely to be included in his will. I know this because Viktor trusted me implicitly and wanted me to know everything about his personal affairs, so I had access to his financial statements, accounts, investments, and even his will. In going through his expenses, I noticed monthly billings from his accountant, and I knew he only saw the accountant during the tax preparation season. Though the accountant's local office was directly across the street from my office, his primary place of business was forty-five miles away, so why the regular billings?

The office manager, Doris Kappler, always welcomed Viktor, as he had a habit of just popping in to visit and pass time. He liked her so well, considered her trustworthy, gave her a key to the lodge to use any time it was available, and—I'm sure unknown to her—included her in his will. What Viktor didn't understand, nor was he told, was that Doris put him on the clock every time he walked in, generating the billings at the accountant's hourly rate. Her lofty status would come to a very abrupt end.

All members of the condo association were seniors, and only one couple had another family member living with them: a son about thirty years old at the time, a guy with nervous, darting eyes. He also had the worst set of teeth I'd ever seen. It looked like someone took a handful of teeth, shook them in a dice box, and threw them into his mouth. This was Ratz, a laborer at a local manufacturing company. When his parents sold their unit, Ratz was without a place to live, so he went to Viktor, and Viktor, the kind soul, offered him an older house to rent at almost a token rate.

It wasn't long before the old place had been completely renovated at Viktor's expense, inside and out, so Ratz now had something of a palace. I believe this was the opening Ratz found to further enhance his position from Viktor's generosity.

I wondered if Ratz was stalking Viktor, because he just popped in too often when I was with Viktor for it to be a coincidence, whether it was in the social room or in Viktor's unit. Hilda saw what was going on and didn't like it. Hilda may have liked everybody, but she absolutely detested Ratz. He knew it but didn't care, as long as he was "in" with Viktor.

I never knew if Hilda was compensated for her services, but she seemed to be present whenever I went there. She prepared all of his meals and did his laundry, housekeeping, and grocery shopping. One day while Viktor was away, Hilda caught Ratz in Viktor's office, going through Viktor's desk and file drawers. She reported this to Viktor's nephew, Freida's son, who had been given power of attorney for Viktor's affairs and, I believe, was also executor of his will. As a result, a restraining order was issued to Ratz to bar him from entering Viktor's personal space and to avoid contact with him. Of course, Ratz had ways of working around the order, because Viktor could still come to him.

Somehow, Ratz had acquired two condo units and attempted to buy a third one, but the association rules didn't allow one party to own more than two, and Ratz, now president of the association, wanted the restriction waived. Over Hilda's dead body! She was upset with the other members because they simply went along with whatever Ratz wanted, but Hilda was adamant that the rules should be followed, and the request was denied.

How could he afford to buy all these properties as a blue collar worker? In addition, he now was driving a new Ford 250 truck. This may have been a clue: One day a $45,000 speed boat appeared in Viktor's garage and I knew that wasn't Viktor's thing, so I asked him what the deal was. He said, "Oh, Ratz wants me to buy it for him." At least this time, Viktor refused, and a week later the boat was gone.

Then another question arose over some real estate transactions when Hilda found a six-page listing of them between Ratz and the Weiners. So Ratz must have won favor with Marie, too. Hilda gave me the list, which only showed the transactions by number, with no descriptions or addresses. I intended to see the city clerk for information, as that is open to the public, but I inadvertently discarded the listing with other office files I was cleaning out after I sold my house.

Viktor wanted Janet and me to take a vacant condo in the worst way. He said he would stipulate that any unpaid balance in the event of his death before the land contract was satisfied would be forgiven. He always preferred to deal with land contracts, as they were shorter-term, and recovery of property was more direct in the event of default. We thanked Viktor but told him we weren't ready for condo living yet.

I personally witnessed just how brazen Ratz could be. Viktor had to take a driver's test, and I went with him to the Department of Motor Vehicles. The test was on a touch screen, and Viktor had never been in front of a computer before. His hands were all over the screen, and of course, it showed wrong answers. An agent called to me, "Hey, you can't help him." I said I wasn't helping but just standing behind to watch.

Fortunately, the DMD manager happened to be standing nearby and heard what was going on. She came over and took us into her office. She said she would personally give the test to Viktor the following week in her office and would also do the road test with him.

I made a set of flash cards with all the traffic signs and went over to Viktor's every afternoon to drill him. One day as we were practicing, Ratz came in and grabbed the card out of my hand. He said, "Oh, Viktor. Let me help you. I'm your son, and you're my father. I love you, Viktor. I'm your son, and you're my father." Then he put his arm around Viktor's neck, although Viktor didn't like to be touched, and said once more, "Viktor, I love you." How sickening. How shameless. How desperate can a person be? How could Viktor allow himself to be bamboozled like this?

Viktor was happiest when spending time at the lodge, which was just under a hundred miles away. We'd leave on Friday afternoon and stay until Sunday afternoon. On the way, we always stopped at Maplewood Meats on Highway 29, a short distance out of Green Bay. It was one unbelievable market for its great size and products available. It had forty employees, and the parking lot was always full despite being out in the country. We picked up bratwurst, steaks, and ground beef, as well as some impulse purchases we couldn't resist.[3*]

Of course, we always had an ample supply of onions and potatoes on hand. Viktor didn't know the first thing about cooking, but he sure did love to eat, and my potato salad was another thing he couldn't get enough of.

We always went to church at St. Jacobi Lutheran, a country parish outside of Shawano, and it was always packed. I would have liked the pastor for my home church, as he was so connected with the congregation, gave wonderful sermons, and had a wonderful singing voice to boot. St. John's in Shawano was the largest Lutheran church in Wisconsin with five pastors, but we liked the warmth and closeness of St. Jacobi. Viktor and Marie always went there, too.

---

[3] * Another really great and large meat market is Meisfeld's, located right in Sheboygan. It offers award-winning gourmet hams, sausages, and about thirty varieties of bratwurst sausages, and attracts customers from all over.

The popularity of a pastor is a hard thing to contain, and it came as no surprise when he received a call from Colorado Springs. The congregation breathed that proverbial sigh of relief when he returned the call, because they didn't want to lose him—plus, they had a fund drive in progress to build a new church.

One Sunday as we arrived at the church, Viktor handed me his billfold and told me to take out money for the offering. Not knowing what he wanted to give, I took out a gmall bill, which he put back and pulled out a yet smaller one. That surprised me, because I knew he was a major donor at our home church, but perhaps that was the difference.

I said to Viktor after the service, "You know St. Jacobi has plans to build a new church. Wouldn't it be a great memorial for Marie if you gave twenty or twenty-five thousand in her name?" That didn't fly with him.

Janet didn't always go with us to Legend Lake, because I think she was rather bored with the slow pace of living. But she didn't mind if I went, as it was just for a couple of days, and sometimes she worked weekends at Penney's during the earlier years.

There was something of an incident the last time she went along. Unfortunately, she was now in the early stage of Alzheimer's disease and had a habit of getting up during the night and roaming around the house when she became sleepless. I was awakened by yelling and screaming from the other side, where Viktor slept. Janet had become confused and climbed into Viktor's bed, thinking she was back with me.

A more memorable time prior to this came when Viktor invited my entire family to spend a weekend at the lodge. Janet, all my children, daughter-in-law, sons-in-law, and grandchildren were there—twenty in all—and Viktor really enjoyed hosting us. There were ample sleeping accommodations, and I did most of the cooking. I had a recipe for a great-tasting breakfast casserole to start the day with.

I was a little concerned that Viktor might not be comfortable having children around, but he delighted in watching them exploring and having fun. He really bonded with my younger daughter, who is very gregarious. She thought Viktor was just wonderful.

The only negative for me was when I found a closet full of Ratz's clothes in the other front bedroom. Oddly, I thought, there were no clothes for his wife, and I knew he spent a lot of weekends there when Viktor didn't go himself. So, Ratz had moved in. No doubt he expected to eventually have the property for himself, one way or another.

Now, I have no idea what prompted this, but out of the clear blue, Viktor announced he was selling the lodge on Skylark Lane. Was it to keep it out of Ratz's hands? Who knows? The listing was for just under $500,000, and it sold within a few weeks. I didn't expect to handle the entire proceeds for Viktor, although he may have agreed to that, but I didn't ask, as I figured his trust officer would convince him to change his mind. I wrote a letter to the trust officer confirming Viktor's agreement for me to handle 50 percent of the net proceeds and listed the performance of all the investments I had made for Viktor so the trust officer couldn't raise an objection there. I was confident the bank couldn't match it with its ultra-conservative style.

Based on prior experience, I shouldn't have been so surprised when I received a check for only $50,000 from the trust officer, with a comment that it was a finder's fee for bringing Viktor to him. Again, I didn't question it with Viktor.

As treasurer of the cemetery association, I met with the cemetery sexton every Friday, usually just before lunch when he brought in the proceeds from the sales of crypts, niches, lots, urns, markers, and headstones. All these transactions resulted in a lot of postings to the cemetery log books. The books were kept at the church, and it was kind of laborious at times trying to locate a property in one of the logs while trying to decipher some of the handwriting in the 150-year-old books, but that's beside the point I want to make here.

Almost without fail, Ratz would come into the bank while I was there to make the cemetery deposit—usually late Friday afternoon. Ratz didn't speak to me and carried a briefcase as I watched him enter an inner office with a bank officer. I couldn't help but wonder just how much of Viktor's assets he had been persuaded to give to his "son."

The latest indication of how well Ratz was prospering came when he bought a new Ford 250 truck. Viktor drove one of those old half-mile-long Cadillacs. I can still see him and Marie driving around in it, and he could have put collector plates on his pickup truck, too. I wondered if Ratz knew—he likely did—how large a slab of Viktor's wealth would come his way upon Viktor's demise.

Viktor always expressed appreciation whenever we met to review the overall status of his financial affairs, and I would review all of his accounts and annuities. He liked to be reassured that he had no financial worries and sometimes seemed surprised at what he had, because he wondered if he had any money. I think he had to physically see or hold something in his hands to understand.

As we were winding up one of these sessions, I complimented Viktor on his book of variable annuities, all invested in stocks and mutual funds that were performing well. He insisted that I should select one. I thanked him but said I couldn't do that, as I wasn't after that, but he wouldn't take no for an answer. He said, "Come on, pick one. Any one."

Well, I picked the second smallest of the five, which was still worth nearly $300,000, but I told him I didn't want it now and would accept it only if he died before I did. It would have been a simple matter to submit a change of beneficiary to the insurance company, but that might have been deemed a conflict of interest, and I felt better about running the change through his trust officer. That was a foolish thought, knowing the trust officer as I did. Viktor did make the appointment and told the trust officer what he wanted to happen. As always, the trust officer dismissed me so he could speak to Viktor in private.

Viktor didn't mention it afterward, and I didn't ask any questions. It was after Viktor died that I realized the trust officer had persuaded him not to go ahead with the change. That wasn't the trust officer's right, in my opinion, as his purpose was to carry out the will of the client and not otherwise direct or influence the distribution of assets.

I decided to sue the trust officer for failure to follow his client's instructions and to try to have the annuity provision put in place according to Viktor's wish. I went to four different lawyers, and each told me the same thing: there's no precedent for suing a trust officer. A woman can sue McDonald's when she spills hot coffee in her own lap, and a man in Seattle can sue a cleaners for a million dollars because it lost a pair of his trousers, but I can't sue a trust officer for acting as though he knew better than the client did. Could it be that the lawyers didn't want to risk getting in bad standing with the bank?

This wouldn't have bothered me to this extent had I not felt Viktor truly wanted it, and it was only a tiny portion of his estate. The only reason Viktor had this trust officer in the first place was because Viktor detested the previous trust officer, who was a young, cocky smart-ass. I initially met him at Viktor's when the trust officer was there to conduct a review of Viktor's affairs. When Viktor asked him a question, the answer was, "Viktor, you don't have to know that."

I think he actually embarrassed Viktor, and I piped up, "Sir, we are talking about Viktor's personal business, and he has a right to ask any question he may have and to expect a reasonable answer." Oh, I just made another friend! I was excluded from subsequent meetings but did meet the jerk under another circumstance.

Viktor came up to my office on a Thursday afternoon, and I was free. Regardless of the situation or event, whenever it came to making a decision, Viktor always liked to get a second opinion, even though he trusted you implicitly, and that is what he was looking for that day. Here he showed me a ten-year land contract that was filled out but unsigned for the sale of the apartment complex he had built on the parking ramp. The buyer listed was none other than Ratz.

I said, "Viktor, if you're going to sell, why don't you sell it to me?" Only 50 percent of the then rental income would have paid off the contract in ten years, a mighty good deal. He left, concluding that he didn't want to sell, but Ratz was pushing for it. I didn't give it any further thought.

Come Monday morning, Viktor was back. He asked me to come along with him to his lawyer's office. And who's sitting with the lawyer as we walked in but the smart-ass trust officer! Viktor said to the lawyer, "Bill, I don't want to sell the apartments."

"Too late, Viktor. It's a done deal," said the lawyer.

After a lengthy pause, Viktor, clearly overwrought, asked about another property he owned, the old Hayssen building he had bought for $2,000,000. For an unknown reason, Viktor had concerns about that property, too. Bill told him he didn't have the records there but would call him soon, and he did, saying, "Viktor, I have the records, so come on in, but don't bring Thomack with you."

I have no idea what the outcome of that meeting was, but Viktor felt betrayed by the lawyer and trust officer. It seemed they were siding with Ratz. Viktor asked me to find him a new lawyer, although Bill had represented him for many years. The first two lawyers we approached declined because they already represented Ratz, and dealing with Viktor would create a conflict of interest. It seemed Viktor's world was collapsing, and he was bewildered.

The lawyer Viktor did retain was an older fellow I had dealt with years before, and he was responsible for the choice of a new trust officer, as Viktor was done with the smart-ass character. The lawyer asked Viktor if he would stay with the same bank if he effected a change to a new trust officer.

The name suggested was familiar to me; my good friend Kelly, who was a CPA with a large local accounting firm, had mentioned the name, so it sounded OK to me, and Viktor agreed. I don't know why the lawyer was interested in Viktor staying with the bank, but shortly after the switch was made, the trust officer jumped to a different bank. The former bank fought the transfer of the major account and charged $35,000 against it in legal fees. The new lawyer eventually got the account transferred to the new bank with the $35,000 restored, but then charged Viktor $35,000 for his services. Quite amazing!

So now Viktor had a new lawyer and a new trust officer, and the accountant was heading to the guillotine thanks to his office girl. Viktor had a few hundred thousand dollars sitting idle, so I suggested a plan to put the money to work. He liked the idea but, as was his habit, he wanted a second opinion—concurrence from another trusted person, Doris, in the accountant's office directly across the street from my office. I asked if he minded if I came along, and we found Doris was free.

I told her that what we were going to discuss was strictly confidential, for her ears only and she said, "Oh, absolutely. Of course, I understand." She listened intently with no indication of her thoughts, and we left.

I didn't want to push Viktor any further and decided to let things ride for the present, so nothing happened. It was several days later when Viktor appeared in a dither, almost shaking before he sat down.

I asked him, "Viktor, what's going on with you? What's happened?"

He proceeded to tell me he had gone back to Doris to talk

about the proposal, and she had said, "Viktor, you can't do that. You don't have any money."

Well, so much for confidentiality, and no wonder he was shaken up. Viktor had dealt with another agent long before he had any financial dealings with me, and that agent's office was in this same building that Viktor owned, so Doris was well acquainted with him as Viktor's agent. How the money disappeared wasn't explained, but somehow it got transferred to an existing contract. Might Viktor have given the agent or even Doris some kind of authorization to act on his behalf without his knowledge?

Doris was history now, along with the agent—neither any longer in good standing. The lodge was no longer available to them, and both were taken out of Viktor's will, wherein the agent had had been in line at the same lofty level as Ratz. I lined Viktor up with Kelly's accounting firm, although Kelly didn't handle the account personally.

Mentioning Viktor's will, I told him the specific designations it contained covered only about one third of his total estate and asked if he didn't want to update it so the distribution would reflect his desires. Why hadn't the trust officer suggested this to begin with? I don't know what happens with the undesignated portion, but I heard it would be distributed proportionately to the named beneficiaries. I do know that didn't happen, so who made the determination—the executor of the will or the trust officer?

When Viktor and I went to Legend Lake, we always went to a restaurant in Cecil, a tiny community on the eastern shore of Shawano Lake. The Cecil Diner was not a diner in the true sense, as it had booths, tables, and stools at a counter along with a dessert bar. The food was always great, with ample servings, and the prices were very reasonable, so Viktor loved the place.

The dessert bar was a delight, with an array of pies and cakes, all homemade. My absolute favorite was the rhubarb pie, which was as good or even better than my own mother made. Five stars!

The only time we skipped Cecil Diner was on Friday nights, when we went to Washington Inn, a very popular supper club right in view of the Cecil Diner.

One night as we were having brandy old-fashioneds at the bar before eating, I noticed Brenda sitting at a table with a man I had met when her husband was still living. I knew the Millses had a cottage on Shawano Lake, so I wasn't really surprised to see her. The surprise was the man she was with: Eugene, also a mason, who was her dearest friend's husband. Brenda and Gloria had grown up together and had stayed close throughout the years.

I had met the couple several times at small parties at the Millses, and I went to Gloria's funeral after she succumbed to cancer. Eugene was visibly distraught, naturally, but two weeks later, he was sharing Brenda's bed, and now they were staying at her cottage. I really wanted Viktor to meet Brenda, so I told him there was a couple I wanted to introduce him to. "Viktor, this is my friend Brenda, and this is Eugene."

Eugene didn't rise but said, "Yeah, I know the chiseler."

I had introduced Viktor to another woman closer to his age whose family owned a long-established furniture manufacturer in Sheboygan. Viktor knew her brother but had never met her. My friend Missy and I knew a nice bar and restaurant in the country midway between Sheboygan and Manitowoc, so I took Viktor there on the way home from Legend Lake. Very good food prepared homestyle and at the right price, Viktor's kind of restaurant, and this is where he met Thelma. Viktor kind of chuckled as he described how, on the third date, as they were sitting at the dining room table, Thelma suddenly stiffened out and slid under the table—instant death.

I had nothing to do with Viktor's next female encounter. The woman was actually a neighbor of his, living in the apartment building across the street from Viktor's place. She apparently made inquiries about Viktor and schemed to meet him by sending him baked dishes and pies. I guess it's true that the way to a man's heart is through food, so Viktor was an easy target—because, naturally, he wanted to know who was responsible for all the tasty dishes Bingo! Virginia Wiggins not only had her foot in the door but in short order was all the way in, as she became the live-in significant other.

She was of middle age, quite attractive and quite intelligent, always reading quality books whenever I saw her. I don't know what she did in the way of domestic chores, but Hilda was not needed for the present. She had other talents, and Viktor was laughing as he told me how often they exercised on the mattress.

Neither Hilda nor I knew the source, but a rumor was in the air that Viktor was terminal, with large tumors on his lungs. Virginia was a suspect. She insisted Viktor marry her immediately, which reinforced the possibility. Of course, that didn't have a chance of getting off the ground with Viktor, and she was out the door faster than she had come in—but not before she grabbed some valuable objects. Viktor didn't try to recover them, as he was just relieved to be rid of her.

Next, we learned that Ratz and his financial advisor from the Appleton office some seventy-five miles away had submitted a withdrawal request for a large amount of money from one of Viktor's annuities. How did Ratz get the information, such as the name of the insurance company, the policy number, and the Social Security number needed to complete the application? What about the signature? Was it forged? Ratz must have panicked after a bit, perhaps realizing he'd been caught, and called to cancel the withdrawal before it was distributed.

I don't know how the discovery of the attempt was made, but as the agent on the case, I was able to request a copy of the application, thinking we finally had something on Ratz. We took it to Viktor's lawyer, as I thought Ratz could at least be charged with attempted fraud or some other wrongdoing, but the lawyer basically dismissed it, and nothing came of it. And Ratz was still Viktor's boy, so he just overlooked it.

Whitey Bullock, another friend of Viktor's, was present when Viktor had the accident. He was fixing supper and didn't notice Viktor leaving. Viktor lost his balance as he was ascending the steps to the door and fell backward, striking his head on the floor. Hilda and I believe he was going to look for Ratz.

Viktor's funeral was just as well attended as Marie's had been. He was cremated and his urn placed in the niche next to Marie's in the atrium of the Garden Terrace Mausoleum in Lutheran Cemetery. The atrium was otherwise bare at this time except for the marble memorial bench Viktor had purchased. His construction company had built the original mausoleum and the second floor when it was added. Two more additions were made while I was on the cemetery board. The first included the atrium, which had a wall of crypts, two walls of cremation niches, and a fourth wall of unadorned lannon stone. The final addition was a long wing of crypts extending from it.

I went to the estate sale hoping to find some remembrance. The relatives had been given the first opportunity to stake claims. Viktor's trust officer was outside directing traffic when I came, and the stumpy critter turned his back to me until I got into the building. What I might have been interested in was already taken, and I wondered if I was going to find anything meaningful.

I went back to Viktor's bedroom and there it was: a hand-carved shoehorn. He always used a shoehorn, and this one was treasured, as he got it when he and Marie were in Africa. It was about twenty four inches long, made of teakwood, with a carved elephant head with little ivory tusks. I have it on my nightstand and remember Viktor every time I use it myself.

At a subsequent cemetery board meeting, I spoke about what Viktor's contribution to the association had meant, plus he had likely been the biggest contributor to the church itself. I asked permission to turn the atrium into a memorial chapel for him at my expense.

With the approval, I bought a bronze memorial plaque, put a stained-glass window over the double entry doors, and added two ficus trees, a pedestal to place urns on during inurnment services, a communion veil to use as an altar cloth, several floral arrangements, a pair of hanging light fixtures, and Carlo Bronti's statue of the Good Shepherd—Christ standing with a shepherd's staff while holding a lamb in his arms. The statue was about five feet tall and couldn't be more beautiful. I mounted it on a plinth against the lannon stone wall just above the memorial bench.

The atrium had about a twenty-foot-high ceiling with a large skylight, and I thought replacing the plain glass with a stained-glass window would be a perfect finishing touch, but I couldn't afford to spend any more on the project than I already had. So I called Viktor's brother-in-law, Marie's brother, and invited him to come out to inspect the chapel. I showed him what had been done and asked if he'd be interested in providing the stained-glass skylight. He'd been nodding approvingly but balked at the idea because his sister's name hadn't been included in the naming and split.

I remembered that he'd been at his cottage next to Viktor's at Legend Lake shortly after he purchased a new powerboat and took us for a ride. Somehow he turned the conversation to the subject of money and concluded by saying, "You know, Viktor, we can only pile it so high."

One day, Steve, the cemetery sexton called me and said, "Guess what? Jesus is gone." We had been experiencing vandalism from time to time. Gravestones and markers were damaged or overturned, but this always occurred at night. The chapel doors were on a time-lock system so were only open during daylight hours, seven days a week.

I wish I had saved the letter to the editor that was published in which I questioned what kind of a person would even think about committing such an act. It was perhaps three or four weeks later when Steve called me again and said, "Hey, Bob, guess what? Jesus is back." The statue was still in perfect condition.

I had already purchased a replacement, so I took it to Sheboygan Area Lutheran High, where I thought it might be mounted in a conspicuous place, but the director placed it in the small chapel there instead. I wrote another letter to the editor to let people know the statue had been returned and thanked the perpetrator for listening to his conscience and doing the right thing.

After my church purchased a former medical clinic and converted it into a ministry center, it decided to start an early childhood training center. This had a large reception area with an elevator to the left as you entered, and just ahead was what I thought was an ideal spot for placing another statue of the Good Shepherd, which the children could relate to. After it had been there for about a year, the assistant pastor called me and asked me to come to by the church.

When I got there, I found him and another pastor friend of his standing in front of the grade-school entrance. They were just finishing mounting the statue atop the school portico. I felt he should have sought my permission beforehand but agreed the statue was very visible and impressive to all.

The following Sunday, a prayer was offered for Hilda's surviving family members. She had died suddenly of a ruptured aneurism while still owning the condo. She had been Viktor's self-appointed watchdog and a most considerate, caring person. When I missed church on consecutive weekends, she was concerned enough to write me a note inquiring about my well-being. That's the kind of person she was, and now her passing kind of wrote the last chapter to Viktor's life.

Potpourri

I forgot to tell you about seeing my old friend, Tom, on campus and walking with a limp, dragging his left leg. I called to him, and he waited for me. I asked if he'd had an accident.

Turns out his fraternity had a farting contest in which he participated. When he ripped one, he tore something.

After returning from their honeymoon, his bride, Elizabeth, confided to her friends that Tom, who eventually became president of a paper mill in Pennsylvania, would blast away in bed and hold her head under the covers. Wasn't that romantic? Does that make him sadist?

During a live telecast of *The Carol Burnette Show*, Carol was standing at the rear end of a horse when the horse's tail started going up, up, up …

I used to watch *The Golden Girls* because there often isn't anything much better during the show's time slot. Two favorite moments:

❖ Sophia never let Dorothy forget she had a shotgun wedding. Dorothy, trying to explain how it happened, said, "I don't know what happened. Stanley and I were in the back seat of the car, and he must have slipped me something." Sophia snapped back, "Obviously!"

❖ Dorothy and Blanche were talking about the times they'd caught their parents in the sex act when Rose came into the kitchen. Dorothy asked Rose, "Did you ever walk in on your parents when they were having sex?" Rose said, "Oh, no! Well, maybe once, but they said they were just playing leapfrog."

Clem, the old Kentucky farmer, heard about a big, tall building that had just opened for business in a nearby city. He took his grandson with him to see this great wonder. Standing in the lobby, he saw a very old woman walk up to a wall and push a button. The wall opened, the woman stepped into a small room, and the wall closed behind her. There was a big dial on the wall with a needle that started turning: 2, 3, 4, 5 …

Moments later, the needle started moving back, 5, 4, 3, 2, 1, at which time the wall opened again and out walked the most beautiful woman Clem had ever seen.

Clem turned to his grandson and said, "Sonny, quick! Go get your grandma."

Something to ponder: Today is today, and tomorrow is tomorrow, but today was tomorrow yesterday.

Did you ever wonder why is it that the cost of prescription medicines seems to be directly disproportional to the size of the pill?

CHAPTER 15

Life Stories

I nearly forgot my promise to get back with more on my beautiful young neighbor, Margaret Moocha, from my earliest childhood days. She married the son of my Uncle Richard's in-laws, Vernon "Snatch" Graham.

His parents lived a few blocks from us for a while when I was about eight or nine. Old Frank Graham was a mean, mean man and called his wife, Francis, names you would not believe: "You lop-eared, cross-eyed, pigeon-toed, knock-kneed ..." Francis, not to be outdone, answered in kind. I think it was kind of a game between them. Frank was a maniac behind the wheel, too, flooring the gas pedal of the big Hudson and scaring the dickens out of me.

One day, when my cousin Dick's parents were away, Snatch called Dick and me into the bathroom, where he exposed himself.

I think Snatch was a big-time high school athlete as well as being the city ping-pong champion. I don't know if Margaret and Snatch had children, but she divorced in time. I never saw him again.

The Con Artist

Kelly, my CPA friend, and I met for a beer after work at a bar we rarely went to. As we were standing at the bar, Kelly noticed a guy staring at us. After a minute, he walked up to us, introduced himself as Gregory Freiberg, and asked us if we might be interested in investing in a surefire winner. I didn't think we looked that prosperous.

He produced a very colorful four-page brochure showing pictures of a building ablaze in one frame and the same building with the fire doused in another. There were a series of side-by-side comparisons. His surefire program was a fire-fighting system. The pamphlet showed amazing effectiveness. The key to the effectiveness was a "juice" for which he had no name. I wouldn't be reporting about this had Kelly and I not gotten intrigued and involved.

Kelly had a client, a lawyer in Milwaukee, whom he thought might be interested, as they had talked about investments in the past. He was, and Greg convinced a former contributor, a dentist, to rejoin the program. After our initial investments, we met regularly, either at Kelly's office or mine, for updates from Greg. By this time, we had purchased a truck, plus a pumping unit from a company in Indiana and a hose reel, both mounted on the truck. Greg used the vehicle for personal transportation.

We rented office space from Viktor's former accountant, so I saw more of Doris Kappler. We rented a house for Greg, and two of his then five children lived with him. I say "then," because his "estranged" wife had another child about a year after we started up with Greg. In addition, Greg was given a weekly subsistence which was never enough, and he would seek out Kelly to hit him up for more money. Kelly usually offered $200, and Greg would ask for $300.

Greg always seemed enthusiastic about prospects when he spoke of things. Although he was never specific, he said that orders would be coming imminently. Finally, he came up with something definite in the form of demonstrations. The first was scheduled to happen at Road America in nearby Elkhart Lake.

The first of two bales of hay was set afire. Water was used to extinguish the flames, but the bale kept smoldering afterward. The "juice," meanwhile, quelled the fire instantly with minimal volume of product, and there was no smoldering.

The second demo was with two stacks of tires. Sufficient water was hosed onto the tires to douse the flames, but the tires remained blistering hot to the touch. A quick shot of "juice" snuffed the fire instantly, and the tires were completely cold to the touch. Those were really impressive results.

The next demonstration was a barn being razed just outside of Port Washington. The local fire department was there, as were fire departments from several nearby communities, and it was another amazing show. The barn was fully ablaze, a roaring inferno that completely enveloped the structure, while the attached building which had been sprayed with the "juice" was not even scorched.

At this point, I thought we really had a big thing going and spoke to a close relative about the potential, and we had another partner who added $100,000 to the kitty.

The successful demonstrations gave Greg some powerful ammunition to work with, and the portable firefighting equipment seemed to be the perfect system for volunteer fire departments, because it didn't require a lot of water, which isn't always available in rural areas.

Nevertheless, at subsequent meetings, Greg had nothing concrete in the works. He kept tap-dancing around about business looking up, and our inquiries didn't get direct answers. Finally, the lawyer dropped out of the group and the dentist followed soon after his departure. Besides his present investment, he had previously supported Greg with $350,000.

Now Greg was looking for more money and asked me to set up another meeting with my relative, but I couldn't do it. He went ahead and made the contact himself, and secured another $50,000. Where or how was he spending all this money? He never accounted for any of it.

Greg wanted to go to an industrial show in Las Vegas because there would be a plethora of prospects there to approach. He returned with none, except he bought a pair of $300 insoles that were to energize him, as he was worn out and constantly fatigued. But there is no cure for laziness. He took the truck to the post office, which was just a block from his office and mine. I walked there, just as most businessmen in the area did. His expense receipts revealed he was living the high life on us, with high-priced entrees and seven-dollar Irish coffee drinks.

There was nother show in Nashville he wanted to attend, for the same reason as the previous one. It was against out better judgment, but we allowed him to go. Same result: nothing but receipts for more high living and multiple Irish coffees at every dinner.

Kelly was now sponsoring more than his share of expenses for this so-called endeavor, so when Greg came to me for more money, I gave him another $25,000. About this time, I heard that he and his "estranged" wife were operating out of another office, so I investigated and found them in a large office complete with top-of-the-line printers and a collating copy machine. They were assembling stacks of 9-by-12-inch kits full of advertisements for annuities. Each envelope had to cost several dollars just for postage. Gloria must have had an insurance license, as Greg certainly didn't.

Greg was convinced he was going to win a big lottery and would repay everybody with 15 percent on top. Kelly and I had been sold on the potential revenue that could be realized here based on the successful demonstrations alone. The venture came to the proverbial screeching halt when we discovered there had never been any hope for it, because there would never be EPA approval. If the "juice" got into the groundwater, it would kill fish. Greg had known this all along.

Shakespeare was right when he wrote, "What fools these mortals be." As P. T. Barnum said, "There's a sucker born every minute."

The last we heard of Greg was that he had resurrected his father's old dairy-products distributorship. The father had been a customer of Lake to Lake Dairy and a constant collection problem, to the point where we finally had to write off the account balance as uncollectible. Greg succumbed to cancer without ever winning the lottery. One can only wonder how much of our investments was spent on those tickets.

Doom and Gloom

My personal-care physician was about to dismiss me after the annual physical when I told him about a couple of episodes I'd experienced where I had difficulty breathing. I was gasping for air when I bent over to tie my shoestrings, and I had trouble breathing in a hot shower. These warranted a stress test, which I had the next day, with my cardiologist also attending. When I stepped off the treadmill, I collapsed into a chair. My doctor popped a nitroglycerin tablet in my mouth, and I was checked into the hospital for cardiac catheterization. Following are excerpts from the medical transcription:

> As noted above, the femoral area had been previously prepped and draped and the patient received a total of 20 ccs. Of subcutaneous Lidocaine. The right femoral artery was cannulated via the modified Seldinger technique and a 66 French sheath

was placed. The right and left coronary arteries were selectively opacidied with a 6 French JR-4 and JL catheter respectively. The ventriculogram was completed with a 6 French angled pigtail catheter. Upon completion of the procedure the catheters and sheath were removed, hemostasis was obtained. There were no immediate complications. The patient received a total of 210 ccs. of iodinated contrast media.

It should be noted that prior to the left ventriculogram that the patient's left ventricular end-diastolic pressure was markedly elevated at 35 mms of Mercury and the patient was subsequently given sublingual Nitroglycerin which did reduce his LVEDP to allow us to perform the left ventriculogram.

Post-procedural diagnosis:

1. Severe coronary artery disease
2. Normal left ventricular systolic function

Narrative:

Right coronary artery: "Dominant". There is 99% narrowing noted in the proximal third. In the mid to distal thirds there is a third area 99% narrowing noted. In the proximate third of the posterior descending branch there is 40% to 50% narrowing noted. There is retrograde filling of the distal third via intercoronary collaterals.

St. Luke's in Milwaukee was doing most of the cardiac surgeries in the area at this time, and I met with the surgeon at seven the next morning for a review of my condition. She explained they were uncertain as to which procedures would be followed. She came in while I was in the recovery room to tell me nothing had been done, as four stents would have been required, and for some unexplained reason, that was out of the question. I don't understand why open heart or bypass surgery wasn't considered, at least to my knowledge. I was released without any instructions or recommendation.

High Water

It was several days later when my mother called at seven thirty in the morning. My wife and daughters had gone to visit my mother-in-law in Neenah. I was standing in front of the patio doors of our luxury condo watching the rain come down. I had never seen it rain so hard; just a torrent coming straight down.

The water level in the reservoir was rising visibly and soon reached the ground level, overflowed, and continued to rise as it reached the patio, which was several inches higher than the sod. The water came over the patio until it reached the building itself, when it was instantly sucked across the room by the carpeting.

Now I was standing in several inches of water. I took my shoes off, grabbed a book to read, and retreated to the stairway to sit until the water subsided. I had to keep moving higher, as the water kept rising. The water level was at four feet when the patio doors exploded, creating a tsunami. The water level crested at above five feet and didn't subside for a long time. The fire department and the Coast Guard were there with boats to evacuate residents.

I refused to climb into the boat. The water was already up to my neck, and I basically swam out while holding my wallet overhead.

The aftermath was unbelievable. Both of our cars were completely submerged. We found our cherished solid cherry dining room set manufactured in North Carolina in pieces, as the water had dissolved the glue. The breakfront had been overturned, as had all the furniture. I did salvage the captain and mate chairs, along with the four side chairs.

The refrigerator was levitating, as it rested on the kitchen counter after the water receded. The grandmother clock I gave my wife for our twenty-fifth wedding anniversary had floated down the hallway toward the bathroom toilets and was lying on its side. All of our clothes were lying on the floor, as the weight of the water broke the rods.

The water was very toxic and acrid from the runoff of manure and fertilizer from the neighboring farm and grounds of the junior high school across the road. Both were on higher ground. This left indelible stains on everything that absorbed water. Once the water receded, we found a half inch of stinking, fetid mud over the entire floor area.

Our losses were further compounded when the insurance company told me I didn't have comprehensive coverage on my wife's car, although I had specified the same coverage as I had on my vehicle. I had just bought her a new Buick about two months earlier, and now it was a total loss. I was driving a late-model Cadillac myself and wanted a similar replacement, which the insurance company left me to find. Nobody had flood insurance, as we were not deemed to be in a flood plain, but comprehensive auto coverage was almost standard.

The flood claimed my neighbor's new Chrysler, but she was able to replace it the next day when Cincinnati Insurance gave her a check in an amount greater than the cost of the new vehicle. Another party was also promptly reimbursed for losses other than auto, so possibly they did have flood insurance. Again, the insurance company was Cincinnati Insurance.

Janet and I moved in with our son for several weeks before finding new living quarters: a duplex next door to the original home we had owned on North 28th Street. So we were back in the old neighborhood we had left nearly twenty years earlier.

Chelation Therapy/Alternative Medicine

I haven't the slightest idea anymore where or how I heard of chelation therapy, but one of my sisters knew a coworker who was receiving treatments, and he led me to the Center for Integrative Medicine in Green Bay.

Chelation therapy is the introduction of EDTA into the bloodstream through the intravenous approach. *Chelation* means to "claw" with EDTA, a synthetic amino acid that attacks a positively charged metal and surrounds it, making it inactive and removing it from the body. EDTA was developed in Germany during its growth in industrial activities, which through paints and other materials caused lead poisoning. Lead poisoning was the original area of treatment.

There is a vast amount of information regarding chelation on the internet. Eleazar Kadile is a medical doctor who owns the Center for Interactive Medicine in Green Bay. I found a brief history of Dr. Kadile that explained his venture into alternative medical applications. As a medical doctor, he was unable to save his son, who was afflicted with lupus. However, with alternative treatment, he was able to save his daughter, who was also afflicted with lupus. He also avoided amputation of his father's leg. His daughter now lives a normal and healthy life. His father lived to be 100 years old.

Chelation is effective in dissolving plaque but is also used for removal of the following elements from the body:

❖ lead
❖ iron

- ❖ cadmium
- ❖ arsenic
- ❖ copper
- ❖ aluminum
- ❖ zinc
- ❖ mercury
- ❖ strantium
- ❖ cobalt

From my personal experience and observation, I can attest to positive results realized by fellow patients. A Manitowoc man was able to return to farming after regaining his vision. Another man was suffering from arsenic poisoning caused by handling treated lumber. A number of patients with diabetes became healthy again. A man who appeared to be about forty years old looked like he would never make it back for another treatment, but after several more, he looked quite healthy.

Personally, there was marked improvement in my health as more and more plaque was removed. I had more energy and was able to walk distances well beyond my pre-treatment limit. Also, all the liver spots on my hands disappeared.

Treatments start only after a complete analysis of blood and urine to determine the formulation for a given individual. A needle is inserted into the hand, and the IV is suspended from a portable stand. There were about one dozen La-Z-Boy recliners placed around the perimeter of a large room. The drip process took three hours and some patients nodned off during that period.

Health insurers did not recognize chelation therapy in general, except for lead poisoning, heavy metal poisoning, and a few other lesser-known conditions. However, others organizations and drug manufacturers maintained that the medical community did recognize chelation therapy treatment as beneficial for the following conditions:

- ❖ removing undesirable metals from the body
- ❖ reversing the process of atherosclerosis
- ❖ improving cerebrovacular arterial occlusion
- ❖ improving memory, concentration, and vision
- ❖ reversal of gangrene
- ❖ prevention and reversing of degenerative diseases
- ❖ treatment of arthritis and lupus
- ❖ treatment of radiation toxicity
- ❖ treatment of snake venom poisoning
- ❖ digitalis intoxication
- ❖ cardiac arrythymia

While my overall health was improving, the time away from my office was impacting my production, so it was like a double whammy between the cost of treatments and the loss of potential income. The Center was over an hour away from home, and the treatments took over three hours. All that plus a stop for lunch on the way home and the return trip consumed most of the day, and I was going two and three times a week.

It was during my hundredth treatment that I was again called into Dr. Kadile's office for a brief review of the latest blood work. I pushed the portable stand along to the office. Dr. Kadile charged a separate fee above the regular treatment charge for the review, and I took exception to that on this day, because I thought he was pyramiding the charges. I didn't like it before, but it just got to me on this particular day. Also, he was pushing supplements from his large inventory.

I didn't want to quit chelation and should have at least stayed on a maintenance program by going for periodic treatments. I resolved to go to a different site I had checked out in Milwaukee, but that never happened.

It was apparent that Dr. Kadile appreciated the finer things in life, as he drove a Lincoln Navigator and wore alligator boots, snakeskin shoes, expensive suits, flashy ties, and the like. I was near the Center for Integrative Medicine several years ago and decided to call on Dr. Kadile. I asked if he had a minute to see me, a former patient, and he did not. But I could make an appointment, which required a $550 payment up front, and there was a three-and-a-half-month wait.

According to Dr. Kadile's history report on the internet, he has transformed his operation to concentrate on treatment of obesity. He developed the KadileAtric Power Principle to help patients end the cycle of weight gain, temporary weight loss, and then even greater weight gain. The claim is that this approach has helped hundreds of people drop significant weight, maintain it and reclaim their health and lives.

CHAPTER 16

Janet G.

R eaders may be wondering why I haven't included more about my wife. In the first place, that would be a book unto itself, and secondly, I had another intention. She was a good wife and mother to our four children, and she doted on our grandchildren. She liked to joke about our fourth child coming as a complete surprise, as it had been almost eight years since the birth of our last child, and I had to remind her that wasn't true, because it was a planned pregnancy. Plus, I didn't want our son to think his birth was an accident. We'd hoped for another son and were so blessed.

I know of no one who looked forward to Christmas more than Janet did. It was on her mind all year long in anticipation as she shopped for gifts for our children and grandchildren. Something for Dad was kind of an afterthought, but to this day, I cherish the special Wisconsin Badger sweatshirt she gave me, which I wear while watching every game regardless of the temperature. She had so many gifts one year that I had to call a son-in-law to haul them to the Christmas party in his truck.

We also had a tradition of attending the Christmas candlelight service at my church, going home for a brandy old-fashioned cocktail, and then going to Midnight Mass at her church, so it was a surprise when she refused to go. I tried to persuade her to go as we always had, but she flatly refused. I couldn't understand this but got some insight several months later, when she told me she wanted to join my church.

I let that pass without reacting until she brought it up again several weeks later, and I realized she was serious. This wouldn't have happened had her mother still been living. I told Janet I'd speak to the pastor, and she said she didn't want to go through the adult instruction course.

I explained this to the pastor and reminded him that Janet had been frequently coming to church with me for more than forty years. The pastor then said he was aware of that and understood her not wanting to do the adult instruction thing. Under the circumstances, she could skip that and gain membership via affirmation of faith, which pleased her. There was a simple rite in front of the congregation, and now that she was a full-fledged member, we could go to the Communion rail together—a good thing for us.

Retirement

At this point, I'm going to fast-forward a few years to when Janet first mentioned wanting to retire from Penney's. That was a complete surprise, as I knew she loved her job as an associate and enjoyed dealing with her many regular customers. Some of her fellow associates were very special to her, especially Sally and Nicki.

From my viewpoint, I was pleased about her retirement plan, because I'd be having a full-time wife again, with no night or weekend work for her. But up popped the devil. She was informed she was two weeks short of the requirement for retirement benefits. It had been an error by the personnel department that had originally given her the date she was eligible for retirement benefits, and the only remedy was for her to return to work for two more weeks after having been off for some time by then. Janet was really upset and refused to go back.

After not getting a satisfactory answer from the store's HR people, I appealed to the corporate benefits administrator without getting a direct response, although he must have communicated with the local office. This was a company error and should have been rectified. A copy of my correspondence is at the end of this chapter.

The company could have waived the two weeks or granted her a leave of absence or excused absence, considering that Janet had given seventeen years of loyal service and had postponed her retirement date several times at management's request. The company president was drawing a $5 million salary but wouldn't do the right thing for a humble associate. While Janet did not receive retirement benefits, she was issued a Gold Card, which she had been told she wasn't eligible for. The Gold Card offers lifetime discounts to retirees and spouses. I still have it, but all the nearby stores have been closed.

Alzheimer's

I got an inkling of what was going on with Janet when I found several pamphlets on Alzheimer's disease, which she must have sent for. I noticed she was becoming rather clingy and reliant on me. She had always been an avid reader—her favorite author was Danielle Steele and she'd read every one of Steele's books—but she no longer indulged in her favorite pastime. I tried to get her interested in jigsaw puzzles but found pieces lying around the house.

My concerns were heightened when I'd come home from work and she'd be gone walking with our copper-colored little poodle she adored and couldn't refuse when he went to the door to go outside. I located her several times myself but had to call the po-lice for help when I couldn't. It was amazing how fast she could disappear. Once a family many blocks away called me to say my wife was at their house and didn't know how to find her way home. Fortunately, our telephone number was on the dog's tag.

I enrolled Janet in an adult day care program, but after two weeks, I was told they couldn't keep her because she was disruptive and always tried to escape—*elope* is the word they used. My next option was for home care, and I had two different women staying with her during my absences. After about three months, both started telling me, "Bob, it's time," meaning time for the nursing home, as they had problems managing her.

I opted for a smaller long-term care facility, as I thought Janet would receive more personal attention; plus, it was important for her to have a private room. I liked the staff, and the food smelled great, too. Of course, when I took her to the place, Janet had no idea she'd never be returning home. I knew I shouldn't have, but I couldn't help looking back when I left the first time and saw the attendants restraining Janet as she tried to follow me out the door.

Alzheimer's is an insidious disease and ultimately fatal. Some people succumb after a relatively short period of time, while oth-ers linger on, depending on the severity of the affliction. I was asked not to come every day, as it would be easier for Janet to get acclimated to her new surroundings. She appeared to be stable in the beginning and even enjoying associating with several other women patients. Her vital signs were perfect, so she was in good physical shape for several years, but then came a rather rapid period of changes. She was no longer able to feed herself and had to wait for someone to help her. I tried to be there every day at dinnertime to feed her while the food was still hot.

Next, she lost the ability to walk or talk and became locked in a fetal position. She hadn't recognized me for a long time, and I just hoped she wasn't suffering, because there was no way to tell.

She had been a resident for four years when she was placed in the hospice care program for people with a life expectancy of six months or less. Janet endured for eighteen months.

It was 4 a.m. on a Sunday when the home called me to say Janet was failing fast. I saw her condition and alerted my family members before calling our pastor. Janet died at 4 p.m., exactly two months from her eightieth birthday. The undertaker said Janet might have to be buried on her side.

We couldn't see her until Tuesday afternoon and were relieved she was lying on her back in peaceful repose, beautiful and looking the picture of health. Her funeral service was held in our church, and the entombment service took place in the Viktor Memorial Chapel. We have a tandem crypt on the second floor of the mausoleum, and I'll be there beside her when my last day comes.

The electronic ministry program at church recorded the church service on a CD, so I'm able to watch it at times that were special to us. It's a bittersweet experience. I know Janet isn't suffering now, but it is sad such a beautiful life was destroyed.

We had our private jokes and I have fond memories thinking about our time together.

My Letter to Penney's

Thomack
Sheboygan, Wi. 53081
January 20, 1989
J.C. Penney Benefits Administrator
12700 Park Central Place
P.O. Box 2405
Dallas, Texas 75221-2405
Re: Janet G. Thomack
Associate #646
Store #1167-6

Dear Benefits Administrator:

This is to appeal the decision denying retirement benefits to my spouse, Janet G. Thomack. The grounds for wife my appeal is that my wife was misinformed about her retirement eligibility and made her retirement decision based upon that information. We carried this problem to the store manager, Mr. Gerald Owens, who has been very sympathetic and understanding but is without power to help. We met with him initially on January 13, 1989, and again on January 19, 1989, when he informed us there were only two options available to us:

1. Janet could return to work (she would have to return all pension benefits paid out).
2. Appeal to the Board of Governors.

(Mr. Owens called with address information today and directed us to you instead.)

We don't recall the exact timing but early last year the local Personnel Person informed Mrs. Thomack she could retire with benefits. Mrs. Thomack was aware of the "75" retirement rule prior to this but at this time understood she would be eligible for all retirement benefits except the Gold Card. She set several retirement dates but cancelled them for various reasons including encouragement from management. Her final decision was to retire on December 23, 1988. Two weeks later the Personnel Person informed her she would not be eligible for the retirement insurance program. There was no explanation. We asked her to call the corporate benefits administrator to get an explanation and this was promised. After a week without hearing from the person we called again and were told she didn't attempt to call because it wouldn't do any good. At this point we approached Mr. Owens with the problem. Mr. Owens told us in our last meeting, "She thought she was right but she was wrong".

This situation has caused extreme anguish to my wife and to ask her to return to work would be unthinkable. I failed to mention her hire date with the J.C. Penney Company was November 17, 1971, and she was an associate at the Sheboygan, Wisconsin location and at the Louisville, Kentucky store.

Returning to work would be awkward, embarrassing and humiliating for Mrs. Thomack, the J.C. Penney associates (particularly the Personnel Person who made the error) the many, many former clients who searched her out and and knew of her retirement and to the J.C. Penney Company itself. In addition, one can only imagine the emotional stress and strain this would cause Mrs. Thomack. We believe and honest mistake was made in this situation but my wife and I should not have to live with it or pay for it. There was ample time for this mistake to be corrected before the final retirement decision was made and the individual who made the mistake is not an inexperienced person in her capacity.

I have some personnel administration in my work experience and I know there is authority in your organization to correct or compensate for this error. Hopefully, you have this authority and can resolve this matter by reinstating the benefit being denied and that is the retirement health insurance plan. If you do not have the authority to correct this error, I will carry the appeal to the J.C. Penney Company Board of Governors which I am copying with this letter. Very simply, I believe the company is responsible for the employee's error and can correct the error by making an exception to the rule, waiving the matter of months required to meet the rule of "75" or thru errors and omissions insurance.

We look forward to your kind and prompt response.
Sincerely,
V. W. Thomack

cc: Mr. Gerald Owens
Sheboygan, Wi.
J.C. Penney Board of Governors
New York, New York

CHAPTER 17

Don

"Bob, Don is dead!"

It was four o'clock on a Sunday afternoon when Missy called me. I can still hear her blurt out, "Bob, Don is dead!" She sounded almost gleeful.

I got the message from Missy because Don's kids didn't know how to contact me, and they went to the Melody Bar for Rita's help, and she called Missy to relay the message to me. The boys didn't want me to go to meet Don at seven o'clock and find out that way.

Don and I became friends in a rather roundabout way. I knew him from church, where he ushered and sang in the choir, but we had never spoken to each other.

Lee Franzen owned a tavern in town, and I had been there several times with Kenny. Lee had seen me playing cribbage and asked if I'd go to a tournament with him at the American Legion Club in West Bend. I had never played in a tournament, much less an American Cribbage Congress sanctioned one. Lee gave me an application for pre-enrollment. Among the options was the Q Pool, which Lee explained paid out according to the standing of the players qualifying for the playoff. I added that fee to the other enrollment fees.

We left for West Bend at six in the morning and stopped for breakfast at Rosie's truck stop just outside of Saukville, where I enjoyed the best American fries along with my bacon and eggs.

At play, I was getting good cards and cuts and wound up as the second highest qualifier from the ninety players. The Q Pool paid me three hundred dollars, and I advanced to the playoffs, where I lost in the first round and got seventy-five dollars from the main pool. I also got twenty-five for high hand, so I had a good day.

The Legion put on a great roast turkey buffet, which we enjoyed between the qualifying and playoff rounds. Unfortunately for Lee, he had to hang around until I finished.

Lee and I went back to West Bend for the next tournament, held at the same place, and I finished as the second highest qualifier again, which was worth another three hundred. I also lost in the first round of the playoffs.

In the meantime, Lee told me about the weekly tournament played at the VFW 1230 club. I was a member of the other VFW club in town, 9156, but never went to another meeting because they and the cribbage tournament were both held on Monday nights. We usually had twelve or fourteen players, and they all split after play except for four of us. John, Neil, Don and I hung around for a couple of beers.

I hardly knew Don when he asked me to help him move. He was living with a son, daughter-in-law, and their two children. I think the daughter-in-law wanted him out, and so he moved in with his older son, who had a significant other. Don told me the boys were constantly borrowing money from him, ten thousand dollars each time. He never got the money back, but they worked off the balance in the form of monthly room and board.

As we got better acquainted, I found Don to be a very routinized individual, always doing the same thing at the same time or day. For one thing, he always ate the same thing for breakfast on a given day, such as cereal on Mondays, waffles on Tuesdays, pancakes on Wednesdays, bacon and eggs on Thursdays. He always went to the same place for fish dinners on Fridays after going to Bean's in the afternoon for the old-fashioned specials. It upset him no end when the routine was interrupted by the absence of one of his breakfast choices, which the son had neglected to include with the groceries he shopped for.

Don was past his prime now but had been inducted into the Hall of Fame for bowling and for softball. We were about the same size and build, but his legs were even more well-muscled than mine. They were his Achilles heel now, as standing on concrete at work for nearly forty years had taken its toll. His body was fur-covered, and he had the heaviest growth out of his nostrils. I offered to braid it for him. He kept it well trimmed thereafter.

Don was covered with hair all over his body—except his head. He sometimes wore a T-shirt that said, "I was bald when I came into this world, and I'm going out the same way."

We had Don over for dinner, and I served my world-famous baked carrots for the vegetable. No matter how I tried, I couldn't get Don to try the carrots, Come on, it wasn't spinach or broccoli.

Don had a son from his first marriage, which was short-lived. Don hadn't seen the boy since he was an infant but knew where he was living up north, about a three-hour drive from Sheboygan. I offered to take him there and suggested his son might like to meet his father, but Don flat-out refused. There must have been some lingering bitterness, but he wouldn't talk about it.

His second marriage was a happy one, blessed with three children—the two boys and a daughter living in Green Bay. Don came home from work one day and found Barb sitting in a living room chair, dead of a heart attack. He was afraid to live alone, in case something happened to him and he'd need help. Two of his brothers had died of heart attacks, and the third was a cancer victim, so he had that dread.

Don got me to join his bowling team and the church choir. By this time, he had given up ushering because of his bad legs but had over forty years in the choir as a bass. I was a tenor, and he loved to harmonize. We always got cheers and applause when we sang at the Melody Bar. I guess his favorite song was "You Are My Sunshine," but he could harmonize to anything.

When our glasses were empty and the bartender hadn't noticed, we irked him as we sang "How Dry I Am." Our voices blended well.

It didn't matter where we met, Don was always there first—early to church so he could park right in front of the church entrance and early to the bar to park in the closest spot available because of his bad legs.

Viktor had been limping around for some time, and I finally got him to see my chiropractor. One simple adjustment, and the limp was gone. After repeated attempts, I did finally get Don to go, but only after I said I'd pay for the initial consultation and treatment, after which Don said he thought he could walk the golf course, but he never went back for additional adjustments. My chiropractor said he was the only one in the area trained to perform the adjustments and had patients from as far away as Florida, Pennsylvania, and Alaska.

Besides bowling and golfing together, we were horseshoe partners for the weekly horseshoe tournament at the Melody Bar. There was a time I did pretty well, but I hadn't pitched in many years and wasn't the best partner. But Don pitched in leagues and still had it.

We were meeting six times a week to play cribbage, skipping Tuesdays and Saturdays because Don wanted an idle night. We played twice on Fridays: in the afternoon at Bean's during the happy hour with brandy old-fashioneds and in the evening at the Melody Bar.

Don used to sit in the back of the church with his brother and sister-in-law, so he had to walk all the way to the front of church for Communion and then all the way back—a long walk for him.

I got him to sit with me five or six rows from the front after his brother died. Janet was in long-term care then, and I didn't like sitting alone. Don insisted on sitting in the aisle seat.

On this day, Don was sitting in the narthex where he always sat to wait for me, and I noticed his eyelids were bright red and later wondered if that had any significance. Church was over about 9:10. Don split and scurried out, cutting between pews to avoid people to get to the side aisle and the elevator. He raced home to have breakfast and then went to Denny's Bar, his miniature bowling team sponsor.

The bar had only two parking spots, which were full this day, as was often the case, so Don had to park in the parking lot of a restaurant across the street. Denny's regular customers got a free shot of booze of their choice with the first drink order on Sundays, which was also when the name was drawn for the winner of the sign-in pool. You had to have signed in the previous week and also on the drawing day to be eligible to win.

Don left early and said he didn't know if he'd see them the next week, with no explanation. He left without finishing his beer. Shortly thereafter, there was a big crash behind the building. Don was apparently stricken and tried to get back to the bar for help when he crashed into a dumpster. He died instantly. It was ten thirty, a little over an hour since I had seen him.

Missy went with me to the funeral home for viewing and visitation. She usually came to the Melody Bar when Don and I were there, so she knew him rather well, too. She was a fun girl to do things with, just as a friend.

It didn't look like Don in the casket. He seemed bloated, and I had to look at him from several angles to recognize him.

Don's kids asked me if Don had a favorite hymn. The choir had recently sung, "Lord, Take My Hand and Lead Me," and Don told me at cribbage afterward it was his favorite. At his funeral, the choir sang it from the west transept instead of from the balcony:

Lord, take my hand and lead me upon life's way.
Direct, protect, and feed me from day to day.
Without your grace and favor I go astray
So take my hand, O Savior, and lead the way.
Lord, when the tempest rages I need not fear
For You, the Rock of Ages, are always near.
Close by my side abiding, I fear no foe,
For when Your hand is guiding in peace I go.
Lord, when the shadows lengthen
and night has come,
I know that You will strengthen
my steps toward home.
And nothing can impede me, O Blessed Friend!
So take my hand and lead me unto the end.
—*Julie von Hausman, 1825–1901*

When the family went back to the narthex for the final viewing and prayer, the sons pulled me out of my pew, insisting I join them because I was part of the family. When the service ended, the church bell tolled once for every year of Don's life. The entombment service was held at the mausoleum, and Don was placed in his crypt, which was just a few feet from ours. So when I visit Janet, I stop by Don to reminisce a bit.

At the post-funeral luncheon, Don's sons repeated that I was family and said they were going to have me over for dinner and take me golfing. It was five years later when the bartender put a beer in front of me, compliments of the gentleman at the end of the bar. It was Don's younger son and daughter-in-law. I walked over to greet them and have never seen them since.

It was difficult to lose Janet, but at least her passing was a matter of time, and we were somewhat prepared for it. Don's sudden death was a shock, creating a void and putting a hole in my heart. It was just three months after Janet died.

Oops! Church Bulletin Bloopers

❖ A bean supper will be held Saturday evening in the church basement. Music will follow.

❖ A songfest was hell at the Methodist church Wednesday.

❖ Eight new choir robes are currently needed, due to the addition of several new members and the deterioration of some older ones.

❖ For those who have children and don't know it, we have a nursery downstairs.

❖ Mrs. Johnson will be entering the hospital for testes.

❖ Please join us as we show our support for Amy and Alan in preparing for the girth of their first child.

❖ Scouts are saving aluminum cans, bottles, and other items to recycle. Proceeds will be used to cripple children.

❖ The church is glad to have with us today as our guest minister the Rev. Shirley Green, who has Mrs. Green with him. After the service, we request all remain for the Hanging of the Greens.

❖ The ladies of the church have cast off clothing of every kind, and they may be seen in the basement on Friday afternoon.

❖ The Low Esteem Support Group will meet Thursday at 7 p.m. Please use the back door.

❖ The pastor would appreciate it if the ladies of the congregation would lend him their electric girdles for the pancake breakfast next Sunday morning.

❖ The rosebud on the altar this morning is to announce the birth of David Alan Bolzer, the sin of Rev. and Mrs. Julius Bolzer.

❖ This being Easter Sunday, we will ask Mrs. Lewis to come forward and lay an egg on the altar.

❖ Thursday at 5:00 p.m. there will be a meeting of the Little Mothers club. All those wishing to become little mothers, please meet the pastor in his study.

❖ Thursday at 4:00 p.m. there will be an ice cream social. All ladies giving milk are asked to come early.

❖ Weight Watchers will meet at 7:00 p.m. at the First Presbyterian church. Please use the large double doors at the side entrance.

❖ The Lutheran Men's Group will meet at 6:00 p.m. Steak, mashed potatoes, green beans, bread, and dessert will be served for a nominal feel.

CHAPTER 18

Life Is Full of Surprises

I'm in a quandary now: Should I end this or continue on? I've received countless "Bless your heart" messages, so I was getting little encouragement to proceed, but an inner voice told me there might be some benefit for those looking for hope when they encounter dark periods in their lives if I were to continue on. The human body is an enigma in that it can be so fragile and yet so incredibly resilient.

A person's health issues can be of genuine concern to people who are close to a stricken individual. Some people just have a fascination with other people's problems, and then there are those who simply have a morbid interest in them.

It was almost twenty years since I'd quit the chelation therapy when I began to have a reoccurrence of the issues with blockage. Nothing showed up during a routine physical exam, but I expressed concern about several things to my doctor, and he scheduled another stress test that confirmed my apprehension. He didn't want a local doctor to perform the procedure and referred me to a doctor in Green Bay.

The doctor was quite young, very handsome, and very distant.

He didn't rise to greet me either, but I wasn't there for a social visit and remembered he had been recommended by my doctor, whom I trusted. I was given the option of having the procedure done at St. Mary's or at St. Vincent's. Bellin, the other large hospital in Green Bay, was out of network.

I was scheduled for the procedure a week later. The doctor wasn't any friendlier. In fact, he didn't speak or explain what was going to be done. I was fully conscious when he implanted the stents. I looked at him, and he just glanced at me. This took place in the month of May.

It was early in August when I went to bed at midnight, rather early for me, as I've always been a late-night person and seldom retired any earlier. The instant I put my head down on the pillow, I had this sudden tightness in my chest. It started on my right side, shot across my chest, and was crushing me.

I didn't want to call 911, after an experience I'd had previously that had nothing to do with my heart. I was clearing my desk to get ready to leave the office when I dropped a pen on the floor. As I bent down to pick it up, I felt this excruciating pain in my abdomen. I managed to get myself home and fell on the bed all doubled up in agony.

I told Janet to call 911, and suddenly the bedroom was full of people. In Sheboygan, the fire department responds to all emergencies, so there was the ambulance crew plus five firemen huddled around my bed. Almost immediately upon arriving in the emergency room, I was given a shot. It must have relaxed me, and the pain subsided, but there was no explanation for the cause except I must have pinched or twisted an intestine when I bent over.

Disdaining the 911 call, I threw on some clothes and drove myself to the hospital, which was about two miles away. I was gasping for breath, and it felt like a boa constrictor was squeezing the life out of me. I ran a red light as I sped to the hospital, hoping I wouldn't encounter a squad car.

At the emergency entrance, the attendant started asking for information. I told her I was having a heart attack and needed immediate attention. She said she'd get the information later and called for help. They got me stabilized with a hypo, and the pain began to subside. Four different nurses tried to draw blood without success. The fifth one did, but I still hadn't seen a doctor. They said the doctor was on the way each time I asked.

She did finally arrive at 2:30 a.m. After a quick examination, she had someone summon the ambulance, and I was on my way back to the hospital in Green Bay. It was eight in the morning when they transferred me from the bed to the gurney to take me to the operating room, but the heart catheterization procedure didn't take place.

I was back in my hospital bed when the doctor came in to tell me I was having open heart surgery the next day. Yeow! Every time I saw someone with that telltale scar down the middle of the chest, I envisioned the person having his chest sawed open and jacked apart. Now I was just grateful I hadn't known more in advance. The surgeon had studied and interned at the Mayo Clinic, so I thought I couldn't be in better hands. His assistant was a very young, very attractive woman.

My children were there and waved to me as I was wheeled into the operating room. Eight hours later, I awoke in what I thought was ICICU—like double intensive care. The only thing I was aware of was the tube down my throat.

I was trying to breathe and kept trying to swallow but just gagged all the time the tube was in place. I think it was about the fourth day when the assistant came in and ripped the drainage tubes out of my stomach, where I still have two dimples as reminders. My throat was kind of raw from the dang tube, and I coughed a lot, which the doctors expected.

They gave me a pillow to hug when I did cough to ease the

pressure in the incision, but that wasn't doing the job. Next, they gave me a mesh wrap to lie on. It had handles, and when I coughed, I could pull them tight across my chest to prevent movement. It worked much better than the pillow arrangement.

I don't remember how many days passed before they got me on my feet for the first time. I was so incredibly weak, I couldn't walk the little distance from the bed to the bathroom. It was a number of days before I could walk out of the room to the nurses' station only about fifteen feet from my room, and I was never able to walk any appreciable distance by the time I was discharged.

Rocky Knoll

Now the hospital wanted to keep me for cardiac rehabilitation and went round and round with my insurance company to no avail. The insurance company said to discharge me after two weeks, and I was sent to Rocky Knoll Health Care Center in Plymouth, which was about fifteen miles from Sheboygan. I don't know who made that decision.

Rocky Knoll was a virtual icebox, with the air-conditioning set so low while we were experiencing hot August weather outside. I never did get warm while there, although someone left a man's sweater in the closet and I claimed it for the duration of my stay. The aide asked where I got it from, and I said, "Right there in the Dead Man's Closet."

It was about the third night when I had visitors, which I really didn't want, but here were three men from the group I played cribbage with every week, and they came prepared with a cribbage board. I really did appreciate what they were trying to do, but I had no interest in playing at this time. However, I said we could play in the social room, which was about three times farther away than the dining room, which I hadn't walked to yet. I should have taken the wheelchair because I'd have to walk back, too, but I guess I wasn't thinking.

We played game after game until I was so exhausted I couldn't take it anymore, and I called for a last game. Back in my room, I collapsed into an armchair and spent the night in it, too weak to get into the bed.

The food was surprisingly good, and I took my meals in my room for the first few days. In the dining room, I found the long-term residents had migrated to one end, and short-timers weren't welcome to join them. There were ceiling fans blasting the cold air downward, and it was only a couple of minutes before the food on your plate was ice cold. I asked the server to slow the fans, but she said it wasn't possible.

I was at Rocky Knoll for cardiac rehabilitation as well as for vocational rehab, which I found to be more difficult than the physical exercises, which were more strenuous but not as long and tiring as the vocational exercises.

It seems strange to me that you have medical personnel around you 24/7 in the hospital, but then you get dumped unceremoniously into a nursing home where you are virtually on your own except for the rehab sessions. I tried to add a little distance to my daily walks and reached my goal just before getting discharged. I walked through the building to the front entrance, then out the door into the hot air and through the parking lot to get back to my room.

There was supposed to be a home inspection on Friday morning to determine if I'd be able to manage on my own. It was canceled without explanation. Anyway, I was being discharged at the insurance company's direction, and I called my friend, Ron, to pick me up.

I was given a little device to blow into to help build up my lungs. It was just a clear plastic cylinder with a ping pong ball in it. At first I didn't have enough breath to move the ball at all, but in time, I was able to shoot it up with relative ease.

Walking was still an issue for me, but I kept extending the length of the walks until I could make it around a city block. Even walking up a slight incline was exhausting, so I walked in the opposite direction to avoid that. My recovery was gradual but steady, and by Christmas, I was feeling quite healthy again.

Been There, Done That

It was January 10, less than five months after I got out of Rocky Knoll, when I went to bed about 12:30 in the morning, and the exact same thing happened again. There was no warning like back pain, pain in the left arm, or heart pain. I thought, *Oh, no! Not again.*

The sudden pressure on my chest was even greater this time than the first time I was stricken. Like before, I quickly threw on some clothes and drove to the hospital, St. Nick's. However, this time being in winter, the roads were icy, so I couldn't drive as fast, but I ran another red light and made it to the emergency room.

A fellow church member was the admittance attendant, and I said, "Al, I'm having a heart attack." He told me to take a seat in the waiting room while he went to fetch a wheelchair. He was back within seconds, and the last thing I remember was stepping into the wheelchair. I only know what events transpired over the next ten or twelve days as they were related to me.

I wasn't seated in the wheelchair when I collapsed. My heart had stopped. Fortunately, a doctor was present, and I believe his name was Dr. Born. The emergency team sprang into action and got out the paddles to shock my heart. They got a heartbeat after the fifth jolt and called Orange Cross, a private ambulance service.

I don't know why, unless it was for the proximity over Green Bay, but I was rushed to Columbia St. Mary's in Mequon, about forty miles in the direction of Milwaukee. I was comatose.

After the initial emergency measures, I got the dreaded ice bath. Of course, I wasn't aware of what was going on, but the ice bath was to lower my body temperature into the mid-eighties to help prevent brain damage. I don't know how long it was before they allowed my temperature to come back to normal—one fourth of a degree per hour. All this time, I'm on life support.

My kids kept a constant vigil, and Missy came every day, as did Pastor Berg, the associate pastor at my church. The doctors told my family on the second or third day that they didn't expect me to survive, but if I did, there was a possibility that I wouldn't be able to speak or breathe once I was taken off the respirator.

When to pull the plug? My family and Pastor Berg were already talking about funeral arrangements, and Pastor Berg told our head pastor, James Mech, "We're losing Bob Thomack." After some more discussion, they all agreed to "give him the weekend."

After the weekend passed without any indication of me regaining consciousness, my son and Pastor Berg agreed to hold off pulling the plug for one more day. Pastor Berg was singing a hymn to me when they said I began to sing along, so I wasn't brain dead.

I don't remember that, nor do I remember waking up. My first recollection was several days later, when I became aware of being surrounded by my family, including my sister, Gert, and her daughter, Christine, who were here from Texas. Chris was stroking my forehead. In a minute, I felt something coming on. I asked my son-in-law to grab the waste basket and threw up into it.

John, my younger son, was visiting me after this, and I started telling him about the first things I remembered. There was a priest who was huge and had a wide gold collar stretching from shoulder to shoulder with a large cross hanging in the middle of it. He kept going in and out of an office and the walking across the room to the window.

Then a second one appeared, identical in size and attire except his face was that of a Black man or an Indian. He also kept going in and out of that office.

I told John to look up on the wall. There was a crude shelf near the ceiling where the priests had put all my valuables.

I also remembered the surgical team talking among themselves about collecting money to help me pay for my medical bills. I must have scared my son, because none of this was true. I was hallucinating.

I was fortunate to be at Columbia St. Mary's, because the cardiologist was tremendous and performed a corrective surgery procedure. As much as I'd like to, I can't reveal his name, because he was extremely upset over the incomplete job done at the Green Bay hospital when I had the open heart surgery, and he said I ought to sue the hospital. This is why I didn't name the Green Bay hospital I had opted for when given the choice.

I loved most everything about this doctor—his concern, thoroughness, and expertise—but there was one thing I didn't appreciate: he started his rounds at four in the morning and always started with me. He said he was going to write up my case and send it to the *New England Journal of Medicine*, but I don't think he actually did so.

I had a private nurse 24/7 and specialists galore. It was test after test after test, day after day. For one test, I sat in front of a live X-ray machine. Something in my throat was flapping constantly like a butterfly in flight. That may have been the epiglottis, I don't know. I was given different-textured foods to eat, like honey, peanut butter, and crackers, and the technician watched to see if the food was going down my esophagus or into my lungs.

There was a concern about me getting pneumonia. Aspiration pneumonia occurs when food or liquid is inhaled into the lungs, and it is one of the most common causes of pneumonia in long-term-care patients. Ventilator-associated pneumonia occurs when people on breathing machines have germs or a virus entering the breathing tube.

My physical therapist was a Russian woman. My vocal chords were in bad shape from the respirator tube, and I had a voice therapist and another to teach me how to eat and swallow to prevent food from entering my lungs, which would cause pneumonia. A nurse recommended sucking on frozen lemon cotton swabs to soothe my throat and stop the coughing so I could fall asleep.

Another issue I had to contend with was my ribs being so terribly sore, something I hadn't experienced after the open heart surgery. The nurses would roll me over onto my side to change the bedding and then roll me back the other way to do the other side of the bed. I normally slept on my side but couldn't do so now.

When I told my son I couldn't understand my ribs being so sore, he said, "Dad, your heart stopped twice more after you got here, and the soreness is caused by the work they had to do to get your heart going again." I didn't complain about my ribs after that.

However, I did complain about another thing, and I couldn't do anything about it. All my food was puréed, and I was put on a salt-free diet, so you can imagine how appetizing I found the food when roast beef looked like Fido's calling card on my plate.

The Explanation of Benefits (EOB) from my insurance company listed eighteen doctors who had attended me. For the second consecutive year, my medical bills exceeded $500,000, and I paid the maximum out-of-pocket expenses, plus I wound up in the prescription drug coverage gap early on.

Progressive Care

After being discharged from Columbia, I was going to the Sheboygan Progressive Care nursing home for rehabilitation, and they fetched me in their van. Physical therapy was not as strenuous at Progressive, but walking was stressed and stress-ful. Occupational therapy was not part of the program there. Progressive was another large facility and had six wings off the great dining and activities areas. I had a private room with a shared bathroom that wasn't always available when the patient on the other side would fail to unlock the door after use. The shower room was a shared community place down the hallway. Again, my food was puréed and salt-free, so that was depressing and didn't spike my appetite.

Progressive's calendar showed a chapel service every week-day at two in the afternoon—Lutheran every week except the second Wednesday, which was Catholic. My granddaughter was visiting me when I went for the first time. There were only three other people in attendance, and I knew there were a quite a few Lutherans in house from the list of residents posted in the lobby. I saw this as an opportunity to do some volunteer work when I got well enough to handle it.

I also volunteered at Golden Living, where services were held every Wednesday morning at ten o'clock. Golden Living was T-shaped and involved a lot of walking to round up people, just as was the case at Progressive.

I requested a list of Lutherans from the activities director at both places and alerted patients or helped round up those who weren't ambulatory. Beforehand, I set up chairs for those not in a wheelchair, and now we had fifteen to twenty in attendance every week at both places. The number included several Catholics who came every week. After the services, I helped people back to their rooms, put the chairs back in place, and returned the portable altar to a side room.

The activities director helped each week, except she declined to participate in the Catholic service, so I did all the arrange-ments except rounding up people. The priest accepted me as a pseudo-altar boy, knowing I wasn't Catholic, and even had me select the hymns for the day. If he wasn't familiar with a particular hymn, I'd sing it and get his approval. I knew him from going to Mass with Missy on occasion and liked him, and we got along well. Missy went to church often enough with me, so Pastor Berg got to know her and called her his favorite Catholic.

More Troubles

I was going back for semiweekly appointments with my cardiologist at Columbia. He had ordered a LifeVest for me, as I was deemed a patient at risk for sudden cardiac arrest. LifeVest is defibrillator designed to detect certain life-threatening drops in heart rhythms and automatically deliver a shock to save a patient's life. It is worn directly against the patient's skin and has to be removed whenever you shower, and then gives you a jolt when you hook it up again.

I hated that. I've had an irregular heartbeat, arrhythmia, for as long as I can remember, but that alone was not enough to trigger the device. My doctor was debating whether or not to implant a defibrillator, and after I wore the LifeVest for a month at a cost of $3,700, he changed me over to a heart monitor for another couple of months. Actually, I was hoping to get the implant, but the doctor ultimately decided against it.

I would return to Columbia several more times, and each time to the ICU area, where I got to know many of the staff, all excellent and dedicated. The next time was when my personal-care physician called me after an appointment to report to the emergency room because blood tests showed I was anemic. I had two transfusions at St. Nick, and then it was on to Columbia for another hospital stay. The next time was for severe dehydration, for which I was sent directly to Columbia.

It was the second day on the IV when I realized my feet were swollen, and then my hands became so engorged I could have doubled for the Pillsbury Dough Boy. I rang for Andrew, the nurse on duty. I told him I could hardly breathe and showed him my hands. He immediately shut off the IV and gave me a shot of morphine to calm me down.

I don't know how they removed the fluid from my lungs. Later, when I met with the medical assistant back home, she told me I could have passed. I asked her if I'd had another heart attack, and she just nodded.

I was at Golden Living for the chapel service and had just passed out the hymn books after assembling all the people. We sat around dining room tables pushed together for a tighter grouping. I sat down at the table and rested my right arm on it, and my arm flopped onto my lap. I put it back, and the same thing happened. I had no feeling in my arm and realized I was having another stroke.

I got up to leave, and a woman there to visit her father-in-law followed me out into the parking lot when she realized I was having a problem. I was going to drive myself to the emergency room but couldn't move my arm to get the keys out of my pocket. Finally, I guided my right hand with my left and managed to retrieve my keys. St. Nick's was only four or five blocks away, so I got there quickly and got admitted right away.

I got discharged three days later without experiencing any impairment because I got to the hospital so quickly and received immediate treatment—plus I did my own mobility exercises there. I didn't escape entirely without a lasting effect. I can no longer write legibly, and my printing resembles chicken-scratching.

Loss of Appetite

I'm not through relating my medical issues yet, but if you've had enough and want to split, I'll understand. I haven't mentioned the shingles and bouts with gout and will leave them alone, as they are too painful to recount.

About two years ago, I almost suddenly and completely lost my appetite. I had no desire to eat, and the thought of food made me nauseous. I couldn't stand the thought of a beef or pork roast or even a pork tenderloin, a favorite with me. I was taking a ton of prescription drugs, a handful in the morning and another handful at night. The listing filled an entire page. I figured they were doing something to my vital organs and quit all but three: Eliquis, furosemide, and isosorbide, which my local cardiologist prescribed.

The medical assistant became aware of this during my next appointment. She didn't object to this but did recommend I at least start back on pantoprazole to help with the queasiness I was experiencing. I felt I had been overdosed and, after a lot of hesitancy, called a reputable Milwaukee law firm to inquire about suing the doctor. In short order, the lawyer told me I had no case, because people's reactions to specific drugs are unpredictable.

At this time, my appetite is only slightly better. I can eat a couple pieces of certain kind of pizzas but otherwise have no desire to eat meats. I did try a broasted pork chop at a fine restaurant lately and only managed to eat three bites. I lost over fifty pounds in a couple of months after the onset of whatever the issue is here.

Regrets

Looking back, I still have regrets I didn't report Willie's John L. Sullivan antic at Time Insurance to the Lake to Lake Board, not questioning the general manager about the million dollar Land 'O Lakes administrative fee, and not pursuing a lawsuit against the trust officer even if I had to represent myself and be embarrassed over court procedures. I may have found a sympathetic jury, or perhaps the bank might have tried to settle out of court to avoid publicity.

Well, folks, the "Bless your heart' messages seem to be increasing at a rapid rate, so I'd better get out of here while the getting is good. However, I really do appreciate hearing from you, and just to show that appreciation, I'd like to invite everyone to my place for a nice serving of what was Johnny Carson's favorite dessert: Prune Surprise.

Printed in the United States
by Baker & Taylor Publisher Services